DECORATING
FROM NATURE

To Laura and Francesco

Thanks to Beatrice Brancaccio, Alberto Bertoldi, and editorial staff for their attention and professionalism.

Metric Conversion Chart

To convert	to	multiply by
Inches	Centimeters	2.54
Centimeters	Inches	0.4
Feet	Centimeters	30.5
Centimeters	Feet	0.03
Yards	Meters	0.9
Meters	Yards	1.1
Sq. Inches	Sq. Centimeters	6.45
Sq. Centimeters	Sq. Inches	0.16
Sq. Feet	Sq. Meters	0.09
Sq. Meters	Sq. Feet	10.8
Sq. Yards	Sq. Meters	0.8
Sq. Meters	Sq. Yards	1.2
Pounds	Kilograms	0.45
Kilograms	Pounds	2.2
Ounces	Grams	28.4
Grams	Ounces	0.04

Editorial direction: Cristina Sperandeo
Photography: Alberto Bertoldi
Graphic design and layout: Paola Masera and Amelia Verga
Cover: Damiano Viscardi
Translation: Studio Queens

Originally published in Italy © 1999 RCS Libri S.p.A., Milan, Italy
under the title Decorazione naturale
Distributed in 2002 to the trade and art markets in North America by
North Light Books,
an imprint of F&W Publications, Inc.
4700 East Galbraith Road
Cincinnati, OH 45236
(800) 289-0963

Printed in Italy

ISBN 1-58180-325-7

Anna Benvenuti

DECORATING FROM NATURE

NORTH LIGHT BOOKS
Cincinnati, Ohio

NOV 25 2002 WAN

CONTENTS

SPRING AND SUMMER

FALL-WINTER

INTRODUCTION

I have always considered the act of creating to offer one of the most wonderful sensations. Inventors and artists inspire me, and I am equally enthralled by craftsmen who transform vine-shoots into baskets, shapeless masses of clay into perfectly proportioned vases or sheets of metal into jewelry. I would love to be a great craftsperson!

Instead I happily apply my curiosity to the experimentation of manual techniques and develop my creativity in everyday life. A walk in the woods, along a country road or on the beach is a chance to collect small, delightful objects that may become ornaments, whether used for decoration or totally transformed. Even a stroll around town looking at the shop windows can produce ideas and opportunities. I think being able to say to a friend "I made this for you or your house" is one of the greatest gifts for anyone who values sentiment and friendship.

MATERIALS

BERRIES, SEEDS AND SPICES

Most spices come from the Orient, bringing intense aromas and beautiful shapes. Although of tropical origin, berries and seeds can now be found in many of our city parks and gardens.

cinnamon

juniper

dill

vanilla

nutmeg

star anise

ginger

pepper

cardamom

cloves

alder

sweetgum

poppy

ironwood

beech

eucalyptus

larch

pine

cypress

white cedar

California cypress

Japanese cedar

NATURAL FIBERS

Raffia, jute, hemp, sisal, coconut, cotton and linen are all natural fibers increasingly used for decoration, do-it-yourself work and furnishings. Versatile and in splendid natural colors, these fibers when made into decorations can turn even a humble cardboard box into a delighful addition to any room.

THE SEA

Shells, coral, twisted pieces of wood
worn as smooth as silk—the game of collecting them starts
when we are children and remains forever magical. We
treasure them like precious gifts from nature.

GRASSES

Along with common reeds, sugarcane and corn, the grass family comprises cereals – wheat, barley, oats and rice – which feature spikes or ears.
The spike has always been a symbol of prosperity and as such is often included in holiday decorations at different times of the year.

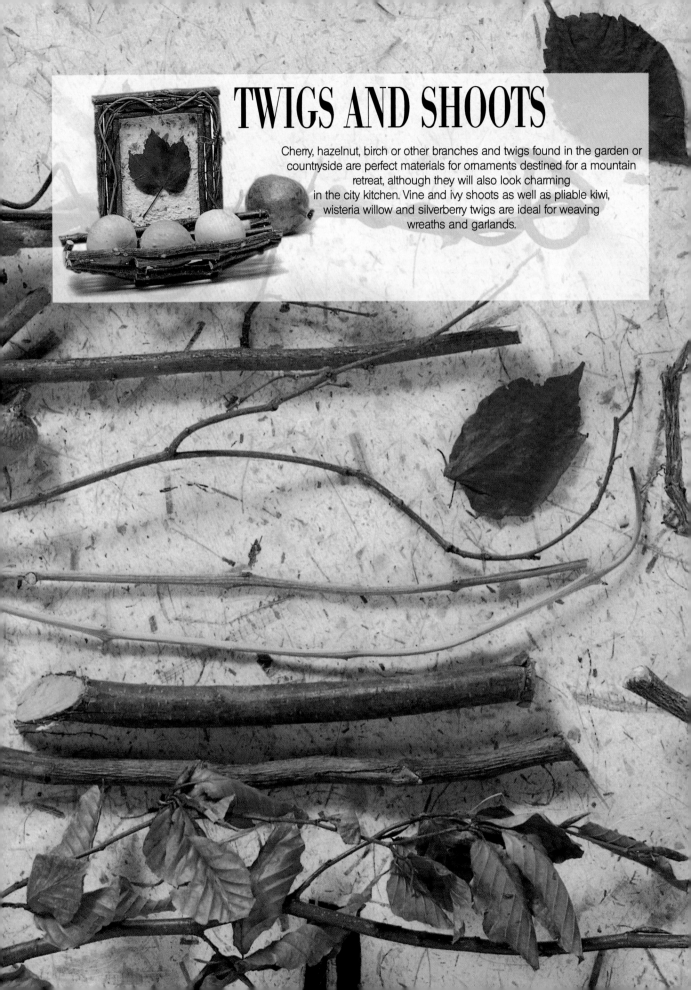

TWIGS AND SHOOTS

Cherry, hazelnut, birch or other branches and twigs found in the garden or countryside are perfect materials for ornaments destined for a mountain retreat, although they will also look charming in the city kitchen. Vine and ivy shoots as well as pliable kiwi, wisteria willow and silverberry twigs are ideal for weaving wreaths and garlands.

TECHNIQUES

PAPIER-MÂCHÉ

Known since ancient times, this is an inexpensive, malleable and strong material that has always been used to create all sorts of things: boxes, puppets, vases, jewelry and even unusual, but functional and original, furniture. Paper (generally newspaper), water and decorating glue are all you need for the two basic papier-mâché techniques. One is based on the use of paper reduced to a pulp and then shaped; the other uses paper cut into strips, which are then laid vertically and horizontally on top of each other and spread with paste. I used watercolor paper for the cards shown in this book; although not cheap, it preserves its white color when turned into a pulp. All recycled paper, even white paper, turns gray once it is wet. The addition of crumbled cinnamon, pressed flowers, raffia, lavender and oregano to the pulp will give the entirely handmade cards an original touch of color. The four sheets you started with can make three cards approximately 20x20cm (8x8") in size.

WHAT YOU NEED

POROUS WHITE PAPER,
E.G. WATERCOLOR PAPER
(30x4CM, 12x1⁵/₈", 85G/M²)
WALLPAPER PASTE (TYLOSE)
LARGE DISH
SIEVE
TOWEL
TEA TOWEL, OR SMALL CLOTH
SPONGES
EARS OF CEREAL (GRAIN),
RAFFIA, DRIED FLOWERS, LEAVES,
SPICES
NATURAL OR FOOD COLORINGS,
OR WATERCOLORS

PREPARING THE PULP

Soak four sheets of watercolor paper in warm water for 30 minutes, then tear into pieces.

Leave the paper to soak in a large dish for another hour. When it has further softened, break it up into a coarse pulp with your hands. With the aid of a sieve, remove this from the water without compressing it. Return to the dish, add a level half-spoonful of paste and spread it over the coarse pulp to make it smooth. Leave mixture to set for a few minutes.

Add your chosen leaves, spices or flowers, and mix quickly. The pulp must be used immediately before the flowers and leaves have time to release their color and bleed too much into the papier-mâché.

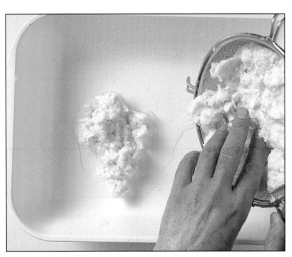

SHAPING THE PAPER

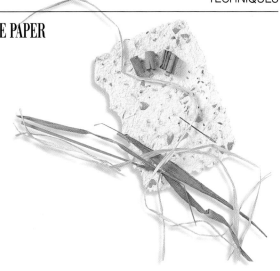

Fold the towel in four and spread the pulp over it, shaping it to the desired size and thickness. It is important to keep your fingers wet so that the pulp does not stick to them. Press gently with a sponge to absorb the excess water. Turn the towel with the paper pulp over onto a tea towel and gently detach the paper from the first towel. Leave to dry completely (to accelerate drying times, place the paper in an oven, preferably with a fan, at 50–60°C (120–140°F), leaving the door half-open and turning the paper at least once).

If the paper buckles, place it between two sheets of white paper in a press or beneath heavy books. Once dried, the paper can be dyed with food coloring, watercolors or natural dyes such as onion skin, saffron, etc.

BIEDERMEIER

Bieder Meier was a cartoon character, created by the imaginations of two German writers in the years 1815–1848. He epitomized the average middle-class German and was the main character in adventures narrated in the German satirical review "Fliegende Blätter" between 1855 and 1857. Later, the term Biedermeier was adopted to define first a style of furnishings and decor, then a particular historical, cultural and literary period and its specific trend based on a choice of simple, somber design in response to the austere, contemporary Imperial style. This same context – marked by simple and practical furnishings – saw the increased popularity of using natural materials such as diversely-adorned spices and berries to create small but precious objects that make the home cozier.

WHAT YOU NEED

SPICES: STAR ANISE, CINNAMON, CLOVES, CARDAMOM, GINGER, NUTMEG, VANILLA
BERRIES: POPPY, ALDER, BEECH, CYPRESS, IRONWOOD, WHITE CEDAR, JAPANESE CEDAR, LARCH
SEEDS: CORN, SUNFLOWER
BULLION (FRENCH WIRE)
TWISTED BULLION (DIAMETER 0.8MM–3MM, $^1/_{16}$"–$^1/_8$")
SEMI-RIGID BULLION
BROWN WIRE (0.35 & 0.65MM)
BRASS WIRE (0.30 & 0.40MM)
BEADS IN VARIOUS SIZES
BROWN OR GREEN GUTTA-PERCHA (NATURAL LATEX)
PLIERS AND NEEDLE-NOSED PLIERS
WIRE CUTTER AND KNIFE
SCISSORS
MEASURING TAPE AND GLUE
WOOL NEEDLE
TOOTHPICKS

MAKING A STALK

In order to secure berries and spices in decorations they must be given a stalk. To do this, use 15–20mm of brown wire with a diameter of 0.35mm. Wind the wire around the berry and leave one end shorter (1.5mm is enough to secure it properly) so that the central stalk in multiple decorations is not too thick. For your convenience we have divided berries and spices into four groups according to the different techniques used to provide them with stalks. Star anise, ironwood, beech and white cedar all have jagged edges. The wire is placed at the center of the berry and passed between the jagged edges and is then entwined on the back to create a solid stalk.

Sometimes two wires may be needed for beech berries placed to cross between the four petals because the capsule often has no stem to which the wire can be affixed.

Nutmeg, cinnamon and ginger all have the same smooth and resistant surface. To create a stalk for any of these, make small incisions with a sharp knife and slip the wire into each incision.

Alder, larch, cypress and Japanese cedar are all shaped

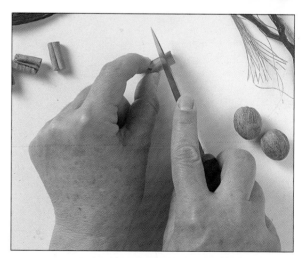

like small pinecones and
the wire can be passed around these between the
sporophylls close to the base and entwined at the side.
Cardamom and poppy berries must be pierced with a
needle close to the base. Because they are so fragile,
slip the 0.30mm brass wire, which is finer and more
flexible than ordinary wire, through the holes and twist
very carefully. If you wish to add a touch of color to your
creations you can also use golden-yellow corn seeds;
stick them together in pairs with fast-acting glue and
then thread the wire between the two seeds. Some
people also use coffee beans; the effect of the latter is
pleasing but there is a risk that the intense aroma will
overpower that of the spices.

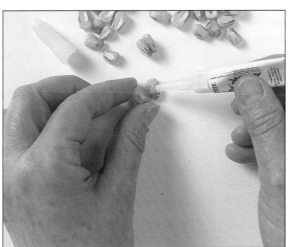

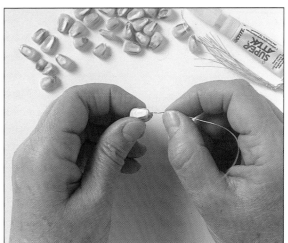

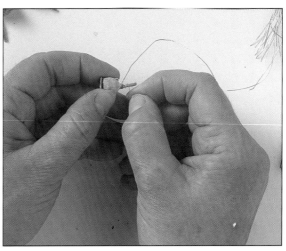

BULLION (FRENCH WIRE) DECORATIONS

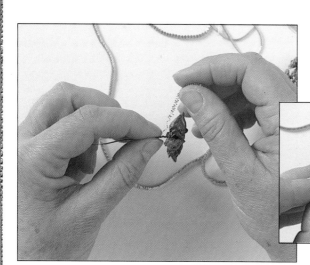

Bullion is a wire spiral and because of its extreme flexibility it can be pulled completely straight, to be secured to a stalk, or only partially so to decorate spices or make ornamental petals. Take some bullion (diameter 1.5–2mm) and straighten it to obtain a 2cm-long wire; secure by winding it four or five times around the stalk just below the anise. Now pull the bullion slightly – it should look like a spring – and pass it between the tips of the star anise. Slip it from one space between two tips to the opposite one, crossing it at the center. Doing this just once should embellish the anise sufficiently but, if you want a richer decoration, repeat the operation. Secure the bullion to the stalk and cover the stalk with gutta-percha (natural latex).

SPIRAL

Cut approximately 3cm of bullion (diameter 2mm) and slide a piece of wire (diameter 0.35mm and 17cm long) through it so that it sticks out by at least 3–4cm from one end of the bullion. Take a toothpick and rest one end of the bullion on it with the wire through it; holding it still with one finger, wrap the bullion around the toothpick to

form a spiral. Slide this off the toothpick and pull the ends of the wire to lenghten it slightly. Rest the spiral on the anise and insert the two ends of the wire between two tips in diametrically opposite spaces between the tips of the anise and twist around the stalk.

FLOWER HEAD

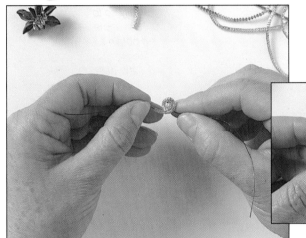

Cut 3cm of bullion (diameter 1.5–2mm) and slip approximately 17cm of wire through it (diameter 0.35mm) ensuring that approximately 5–6cm protrudes from it (depending on the size of berry to be adorned) from the bullion. Now insert a 3mm (1/8") diameter bead onto the shortest end of the wire. Wind the bullion around the bead keeping 5cm of wire below the head that forms from the winding. Bend both ends of the wire beneath the head in diametrically opposite directions. Rest the head in the center of the anise, pass the two ends of the wire between two tips of the anise opposite each other and secure them to the stalk.

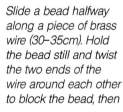

GILDED COIL

Slide a bead halfway along a piece of brass wire (30–35cm). Hold the bead still and twist the two ends of the wire around each other to block the bead, then slip approximately 7cm of bullion over the wire. Use the needle-nosed pliers to form a small ring at the base of the bullion to stop it from moving. Hold the bead still and twist the brass wire covered with bullion spiral around a toothpick. Slide the spiral off and pull slightly to form a coil that will add luminosity to your creations.

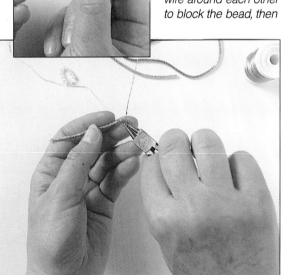
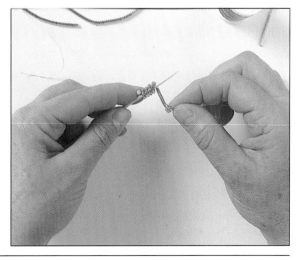

BEAD DECORATIONS

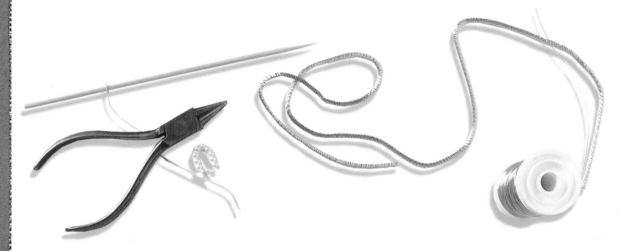

Take approximately 12cm of brass wire (diameter 0.30mm) and thread it with five beads 3mm (⅛") in diameter. Fold the brass wire with the beads into a circle and thread one end back through the first two beads. Take both ends of the wire and pull to form a small crown. It will not be perfectly centered in relation to the end of the wire, and you must take this into account when placing it on the spice or berry. Here, for instance, the crown must be placed at the center of the star anise and the two brass wire ends will be inserted in two adjacent spaces. This small gilded crown will enhance any type of berry.

DECORATING A CLOVE

Cloves used in Biedermeier ornaments are nearly always decorated. Cut 1.6–1.8cm (depending on the size of the clove) of twisted bullion (diameter 2–3mm). Insert the wire, which must protrude by at least 4cm from the end of the bullion. Bend the longest end of the wire into a circle and reinsert the end of the wire into the bullion, bringing it out again after approximately 2–3mm.

Pull the end of the wire to form a circle. Place the gilded crown on the clove and secure the two ends of the wire by first winding them around the stalk of the clove and then twisting them around each other.

Cover the wire and stalk with gutta-percha.

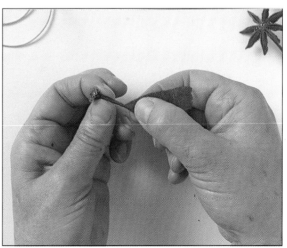

MAKING A BULLION FLOWER

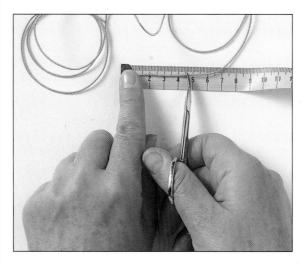

Cut 5x4.5cm-long pieces of semi-rigid bullion (diameter 1.2mm). Thread five pieces of wire (diameter 0.35mm) through them and close them to form a petal. Secure the bullion (diameter 1.5mm) to the stem. Pull it slightly and wind it diagonally around the petal, first in one direction, then the other. Fill any empty spaces by winding more gold thread around; it should look like filigree when finished. Make five petals in the same way.

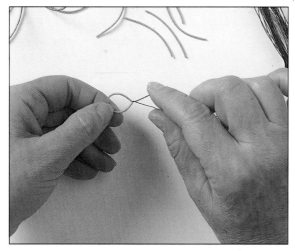

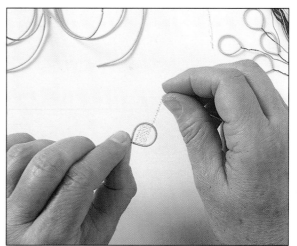

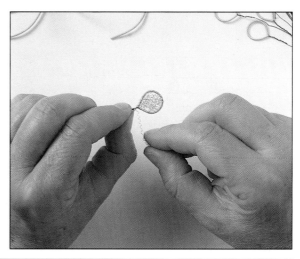

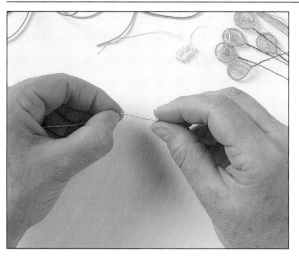

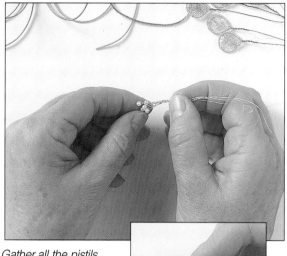

Now make the pistils. Insert a piece of brass wire (diameter 0.30mm) into a bead (diameter 3–4mm, 1/8"–1/4"). Bring it out by at least 4–5cm and hold the bead still with two fingers on the holes as you fold the wire back on itself. Hold the two wires firmly together and turn the bead to twist the two wires evenly. Make three-five pistils in all.

Gather all the pistils together and twist the stalks. Take the five petals in your left hand and place one beside the other, all at the same height. Open the petals to form a flower.

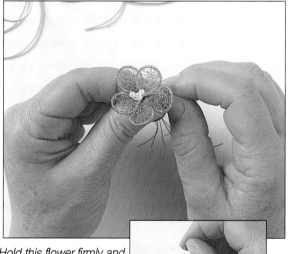

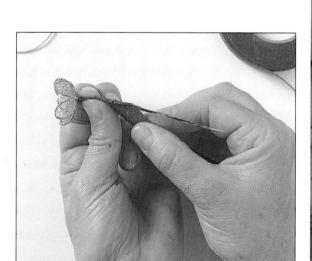

Hold this flower firmly and insert the pistils from the side, filling the center of the flower. Wind a piece of brass wire three to four times around the base of the flower, and tighten and twist the petal stalks around each other to make the stem more compact.

Cover the flower stem with gutta-percha. It is important to use this properly for successful Biedermeier work. Here, it is used to cover all the stalks, especially those that the bullion is secured to, and to bind the stalks to each other. The trick lies in proper pulling; do not be discouraged if it breaks the first few times. You will gradually acquire the skill to do a perfect job.

CANDLES

Making candles in your own home is simple and fun to do, and creating candles in original containers also provides the satisfaction of reusing and salvaging objects long forgotten in the cellar or found in antique stores – odd glasses, china cups or old pottery. Aromatherapy is extremely popular today and will provide you with hundreds of ideas for personalizing your candles. In summer, add a few drops of citronella or geranium essence to the melted wax and you will also keep mosquitoes and gnats at bay.

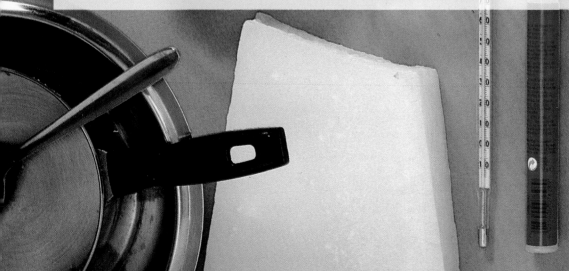

WHAT YOU NEED

PARAFFIN AND STEARIN
WAXED WICK (DIAMETER
2.5–3MM, $^1/_{12}$" –$^1/_8$")
GERANIUM OR CITRONELLA
ESSENCE
SHEET OF PAPER
GLUE AND SCISSORS
LIQUID THERMOMETER
(TEMPERATURE AT LEAST
100°C, 212°F)
SHEET OF TIN FOIL
NON-FLAMMABLE CONTAINERS
FOR THE CANDLES
WOODEN SKEWER
ADHESIVE TAPE
MELTING PAN
DOUBLE BOILER

PREPARING THE CONTAINER FOR THE CANDLE

Use a 3mm ($1/8$") wick for a container with a diameter of approximately 5–6cm (2–2 $3/8$"). Put at least two or three wicks in larger containers. Cut a small square of paper, make a hole in the center with a skewer and push the wick through. Stick the square of paper with the wick in the center of the container bottom and leave to dry. Tie the free end of the wick to the center of the skewer and lay this on the edge of the container so that the wick is taut and straight. Tape the skewer to the edges of the container with two pieces of tape.

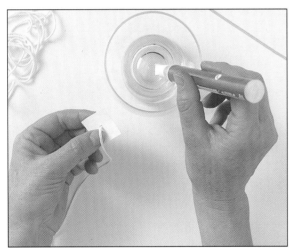

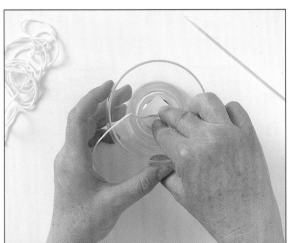

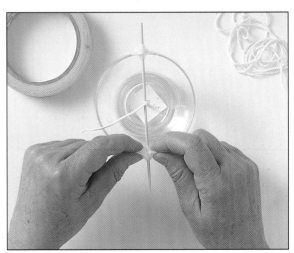

MAKING THE CANDLE

Place the container on a perfectly flat surface and do not move it until the wax has solidified. The candle wax will be 20 percent stearin and 80 percent paraffin. Melt the stearin in a bain-marie pan (double boiler). Add the paraffin and allow it to dissolve completely. Heat the wax to a temperature of 82°C (180°F); it must become completely liquid. Add about ten drops of perfume essence. Pour the wax into the container using the sheet of tin foil folded into a U-shape. This will prevent bubbles from forming on the surface of the candle. Leave to cool. Use the remaining hot wax to fill the hollow that forms around the wick. Any splashes of wax on the container can be removed with a knife and the residue with a little rubbing alcohol or mineral spirits.

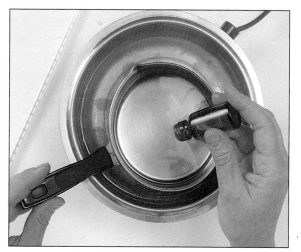

WREATHS, STARS AND HEARTS

These are the shapes most commonly used as bases for natural decorations and creations. They are very beautiful and with just a little imagination you can personalize them to make unique gifts or accents for your home.

WHAT YOU NEED

SHOOTS OR TWIGS OF VINE, RUSH, BROOM, LAVENDER, WILLOW, SILVERBERRY, CREEPER, ETC.
CANE
HAY
MOSS
CEREAL (GRAIN) STALKS
PLIERS
MEASURING TAPE
SCISSORS
WIRE (DIAMETER 1.5–2MM)
FINE BROWN WIRE
RAFFIA

A VINE WREATH

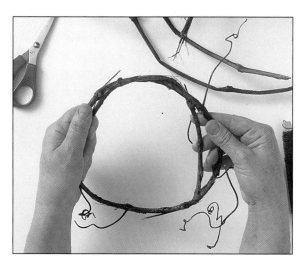

Before starting, leave the shoots or twigs chosen to soak as this makes them more pliable. Take the first shoot, at least 40cm (16") longer than the desired circumference. Bend it to form a circle and weave the end along its circumference.
Wind two or three shoots in a spiral around it. Secure these with a piece of wire where the ends tend to protrude, tightening it well with the pliers. Insert the ends of the next shoots into the empty spaces at the base and wind them around, always working in the same direction.

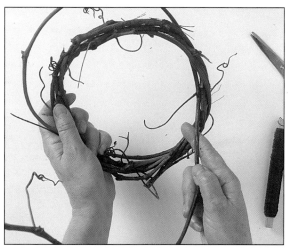

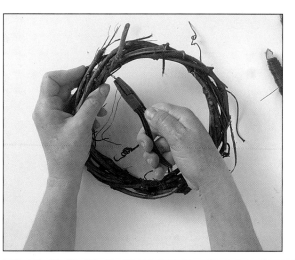

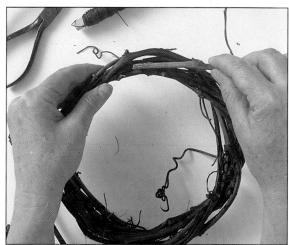

A HAY, MOSS OR CEREAL STALK WREATH

Cut a piece of wire (diameter 2mm) twice the length of the desired circumference. With the wire, form a circle and secure the ends by winding them around the circumference. Take a handful of hay, place it around the wire and secure with fine wire wound in a spiral. Proceed, adding more hay and tying it until the wreath is completely covered.

A HEART

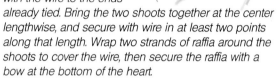

Cut two shoots the same length. Bring two ends together and tie them, twisting a piece of wire around the point where they overlap. Bend the two free ends of shoots inwards to form a heart shape and secure them with the wire to the ends already tied. Bring the two shoots together at the center lengthwise, and secure with wire in at least two points along that length. Wrap two strands of raffia around the shoots to cover the wire, then secure the raffia with a bow at the bottom of the heart.

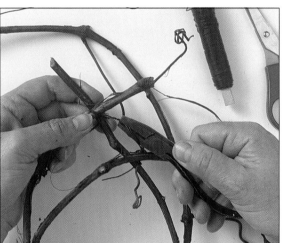

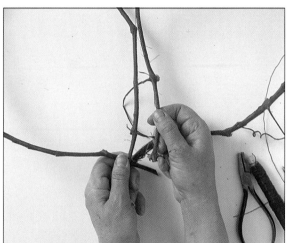

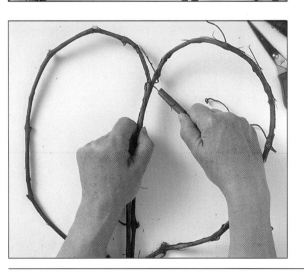

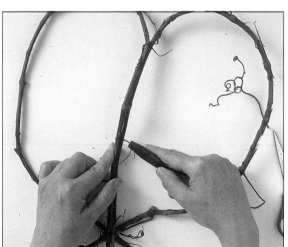

A STAR

I have used cane, which is straight and has no tendrils, to make the execution clearer but any other pliable material can be used for this accent. Measure out 22cm (8") of cane and bend at that point. Form another three consecutive segments 20cm (8") long and then one 22cm (¹/₈") long in the same way. Now cut the cane, of which you will have used 104cm (41") in all. Bend the cane at each measured point and shape it into a star; then tie the two ends of the cane, which will overlap each other, with raffia. For a well-formed star, make sure the pentagon at its center is as regular as possible. Secure the points where the segments of cane cross with raffia.

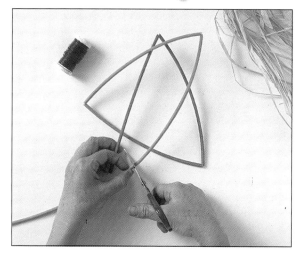

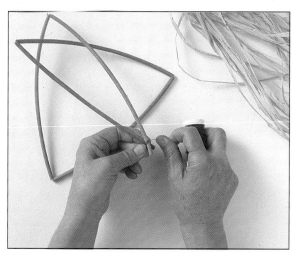

RAFFIA

Raffia is the product of a palm common to Africa and some tropical parts of America. Its large leaves, more than 2m (6'6") long, are used to make long strips of tough fiber, known as raffia strands. This light, pliable and highly versatile material can be plaited (braided), sewn or dyed for various uses such as wrapping, tying or general decorating. Raffia is sold in large skeins by agricultural companies and basketry shops; smaller but better quality skeins can be found in craft shops. If you buy a large skein, divide it into bunches of about ten strands—this will make it easier to use.

WHAT YOU NEED

RAFFIA STRANDS

THREE-WAY BRAID

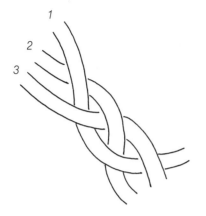

Make three bunches of raffia with roughly the same thickness and braid them normally. Not all will be the same length and they will tend to thin out towards the end. You will have to gradually add new bunches to maintain a regular thickness and continue the braid. Insert these so that you braid at least three times with the old and new bunches together. This will produce a firm, compact braid. Later, you can cut away the protruding raffia end. This insertion method also applies to four-, five- and seven-way braids.

FOUR-WAY BRAID

To make a four-way braid, proceed as shown in the photograph, numbering your bunches from one to four and working from right to left. First braid the central bunches, two over three; then pass left side bunch four over two. Do the same on the right with three over one. Continue this sequence, pulling the braid tightly throughout.

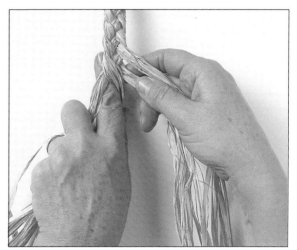

FIVE-WAY BRAID

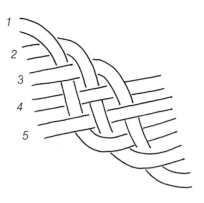

The execution of this braid may look complicated at first but will soon become almost automatic. Follow the sequence of photographs, and you will realize that you are practically weaving with the bunch on the right passing over and under the others alternately. Pass the bunch of raffia farthest right over the first one to its left, then under the next one, over the third and under the fourth. Then start again from the right. The only possible problem is that you may find yourself with a braid that slants to the left. To avoid this, remember to tighten the braid well, pulling the strands to the right. The same procedure can be adopted to make seven- and even nine-way braids. As there are numerous raffia strands in each bunch, you may have difficulty keeping them separate from each other. In this case, hold the strands of each bunch together with a small rubber band and slide this down as you work.

PRESSED FLOWERS

Who hasn't yielded to the temptation of picking a flower and conserving it between the pages of a book only to rediscover it perhaps years later, slightly faded but still charged with memories? Picking and drying flowers can be turned into a very satisfying hobby that produces original and creative ideas and saves you money as well. Plants that can be dried are growing all around you—in the fields, in your garden, even in the window box. And only the simplest of equipment is needed to dry them. Flowers may be slight and fragile but with just a little care they can be conserved at length and used to adorn bookmarks, pictures, trays, notecards, lampshades and even furniture, which, when the flowers are decorated and lacquered, acquires a fresh and luminous appearance.

WHAT YOU NEED

PLYWOOD PRESS
CARDBOARD
BLOTTING PAPER
SCISSORS
FLAT-TIPPED TWEEZERS
TISSUE PAPER

TO MAKE A PORTABLE PRESS

TWO RECTANGLES OF MASONITE
HARDBOARD
(20x25 CM, $^8/_{10}$")
CARDBOARD
BLOTTING PAPER
TWO STRIPS OF ELASTIC
(APPROXIMATELY 40CM, 16"
LONG, 2–3CM, $^3/_4$ – 1$^1/_8$" WIDE
PENCIL
STAPLER
(SEE INSTRUCTIONS ON PAGE 57)

MAKING PRESSED FLOWERS

Flowers and leaves must be pressed while still fresh and dry. If a flower has withered slightly, revive it in water. Change the blotting paper in the press frequently because, unlike cardboard, the paper cannot be reused. Detach the calyxes of the flowers, primroses in this case, and any parts that may leave unwanted marks or signs on the corolla. Choose flowers of the same type and thickness for each layer and place them on the

blotting paper so that they do not overlap. Most small flowers will be dry in four to five days, bigger flowers in two weeks.

Do the same with the stems and leaves which, although stronger than the corolla, still have to be dried properly. The largest and thickest leaves can be flattened between sheets of newspaper with a hot non-steam iron—they will dry far more quickly this way.

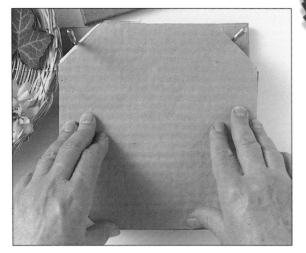

[Alternate layers of flowers, blotting paper and cardboard in the press, and close the press, tightening the fly nuts. To shorten drying times from one to two weeks, place the press in the sun or close to a source of heat. For the first few days, change the blotting paper daily, then every three to four days. The best way to do this is to slip the entire block out of the press, turn it upside down and delicately remove the paper covering the flowers. Lay the flowers on fresh blotting paper in the press and change the other layer of blotting paper as well. When dry, flowers are very fragile; use flat-tipped tweezers to move them, holding them at the center and never along the edges of the petals. Conserve them in boxes, arranged in layers and separated by sheets of tissue paper.

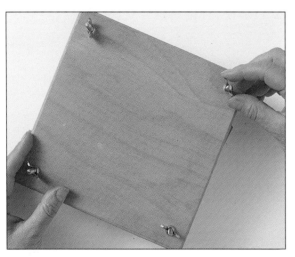

MAKING A PORTABLE PRESS

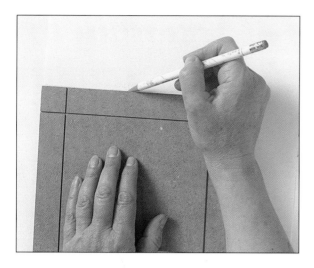

Freshly picked flowers should be placed in a press immediately to conserve them properly. Make a portable press with masonite hardboard. Draw around the masonite on the blotting paper and also on the cardboard, then cut out the drawn shape. Alternate sheets of cardboard and blotting paper one on the other. Overlap the ends of each strip of elastic by 4cm (1²/₃") and secure with four staples. Use these elastic straps to keep the press tightly closed.

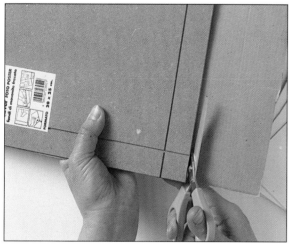

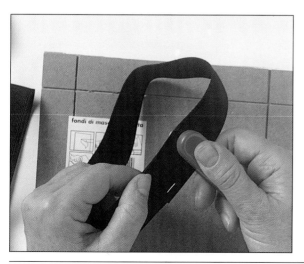

SPRING AND
SUMMER

HYACINTHS IN BLOOM

Spring has come at last! As nature reawakens you can revamp
your clay flowerpots. With just a little string, some raffia,
cane and wood, they will be ready to display brightly colored
hyacinths on the windowsill.

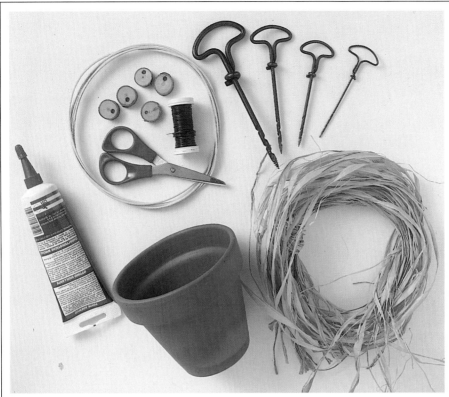

FLOWERPOT TRIMMED
WITH CANE

WHAT YOU NEED
CLAY FLOWERPOT
RAFFIA AND SCISSORS
CANE (DIAMETER 2MM, $^1/_{16}$")
PERFORATED WOODEN DISKS
(HOLE DIAMETER 4MM, $^3/_8$")
FINE WIRE
SIZE 1, 2, 3 & 5 AUGERS
STRONG GLUE

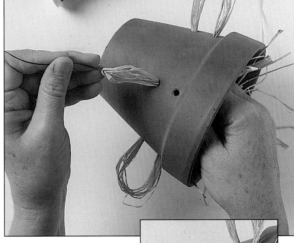

Divide the circumference of the flowerpot into four sectors. Use the smallest auger to make a hole in each sector along the side of the pot. To make holes in flowerpots without the risk of cracking them, they should be left to soak in water overnight. Alternatively, use an electric drill. After making the holes with the smallest auger, gradually enlarge each of them by inserting the larger ones. Make another four holes exactly 3cm (1$^1/_8$") below the first ones, enlarging them with the larger augers.

Pass a tuft of raffia through a hole. Make a loop with the wire and insert a tuft of raffia through it; pass the wire with the raffia from the bottom hole to the hole above it to form a loop. The raffia must be long enough to allow you to tie it in a double knot inside the flowerpot later.

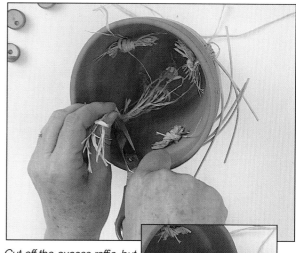

Wind the cane through the raffia loops about ten times, pulling the ends evenly. Pull the raffia loops towards the flowerpot to block the cane. Tie the raffia inside the flowerpot in a tight knot. If you leave the cane to soak overnight before use, it will be easier to manipulate.

Cut off the excess raffia, but not too close to the knots or they will come undone. Secure them with a little glue and use the same glue to fill in the holes.

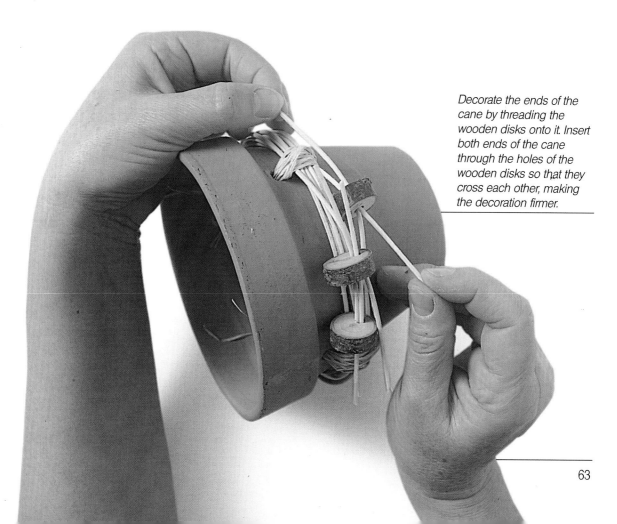

Decorate the ends of the cane by threading the wooden disks onto it. Insert both ends of the cane through the holes of the wooden disks so that they cross each other, making the decoration firmer.

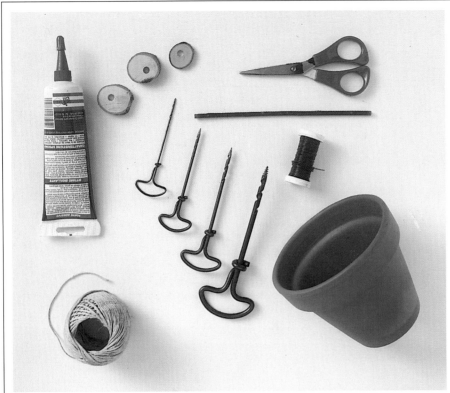

FLOWERPOT WITH MACRAME
KNOT DECORATION

WHAT YOU NEED
CLAY FLOWERPOT
STRING (DIAMETER 2MM, $^1/_{16}$")
FOUR THIN TWIGS OF THE
SAME LENGTH
PERFORATED WOODEN DISKS
(HOLE DIAMETER 4MM, $^3/_8$")
FINE WIRE
SCISSORS, GLUE
SIZE 1, 2, 3 & 5 AUGERS

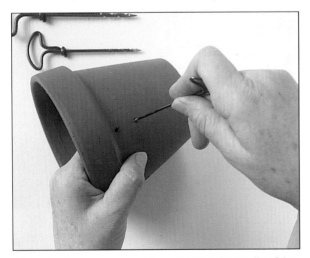

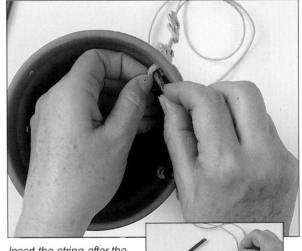

Make four holes at regular intervals along the top lip of the pot then make another three holes (between two of the horizontal holes) in a vertical line beneath the lip.
Fold the string over, doubling it, and make a single knot, forming a loop, then an ornamental knot (see diagram). The length of the single and ornamental knots together must cover the distance between two holes on the lip of the flowerpot.

Insert the string after the two knots in one of the horizontal holes. Place a twig in the loop formed inside and fix with glue. Make two ornamental knots (that fill a space equal to the distance between two holes on the lip), insert the string, again doubling it, in the next hole; slip in a twig and glue it to the flowerpot. Proceed in the same way all around the lip of the flowerpot.

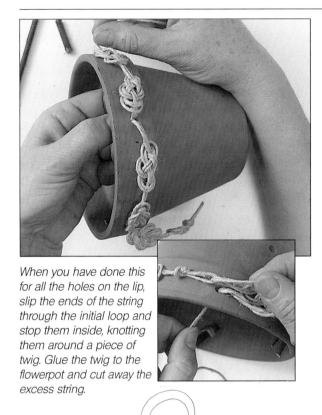

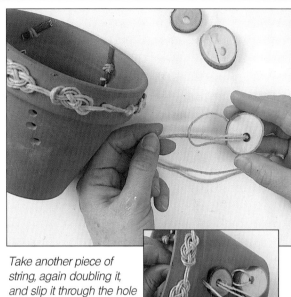

When you have done this for all the holes on the lip, slip the ends of the string through the initial loop and stop them inside, knotting them around a piece of twig. Glue the twig to the flowerpot and cut away the excess string.

Take another piece of string, again doubling it, and slip it through the hole in a wooden disk; pass the ends of the string through the formed loop and pull, tightening the ring. Now slip the string into the bottom hole on the flowerpot. Bring the string out through the hole above, thread on a wooden disk and insert the string into the third hole so that the end is inside the flowerpot.

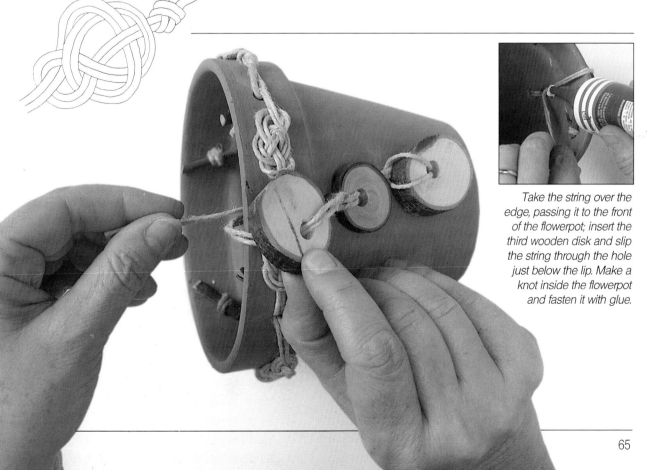

Take the string over the edge, passing it to the front of the flowerpot; insert the third wooden disk and slip the string through the hole just below the lip. Make a knot inside the flowerpot and fasten it with glue.

BAMBOO TRAY

Three delightful bamboo trays decorated with burlap, green ivy leaves, pressed flowers and with a delicate bamboo frame—a bamboo tray is easy to make and creates a striking effect.

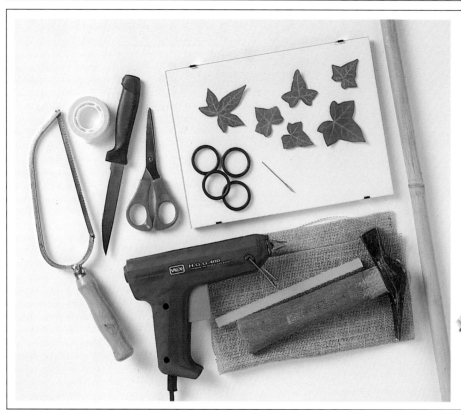

WHAT YOU NEED

BAMBOO CANE (DIAMETER 1.5CM, 5/8")
PLEXIGLAS FRAME
BURLAP
SIX IVY LEAVES
FOUR PLUMBERS GASKETS (DIAMETER 3CM, 1/8")
KNIFE
SCISSORS
HACKSAW
DOUBLE-SIDED TAPE
HAMMER
WOOL NEEDLE
HOT GLUE GUN

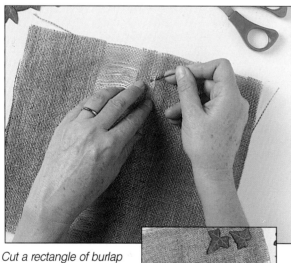

Cut a rectangle of burlap slightly larger than the frame. Find the center of the fabric. About 1cm (³/₈") from the center on each side, draw out enough threads to make room to insert a leaf (6 threads = 1cm, ³/₈" approximately). Use the knife to raise some threads of the warp at various points on the fabric, and insert the ivy leaves.

Stick the double-sided tape along the four edges of the masonite hardboard frame on one side and remove the protective film from the tape.

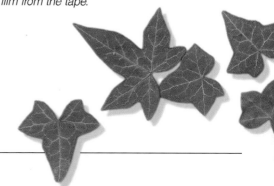

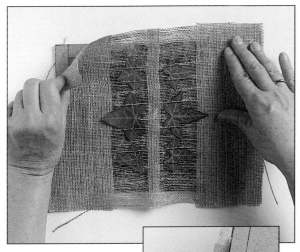

Position the burlap with the leaves on the frame with the double-sided tape, keeping it centered and taut. Cut away the excess fabric; the double-sided tape will prevent fraying. Attach the plexiglas to the base of the frame with the clips.

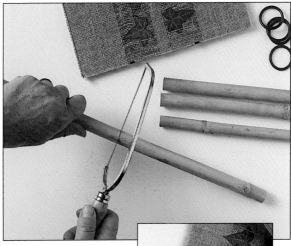

Use the hacksaw to cut six pieces of bamboo at least 4cm (1⁹/₁₆") longer than the shortest side of the frame. Before proceeding, score with the hacksaw the circumference of the bamboo cane to prevent cracking. Group the canes in threes and tie the ends with the gaskets.

Spread a little glue along the shorter edges of the frame and insert the frame between the bamboo canes.

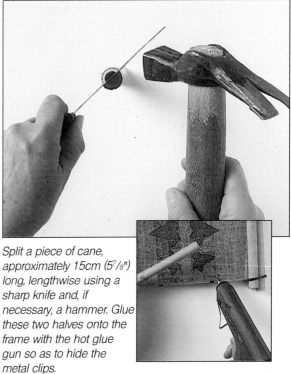

Split a piece of cane, approximately 15cm (5⁷/₈") long, lengthwise using a sharp knife and, if necessary, a hammer. Glue these two halves onto the frame with the hot glue gun so as to hide the metal clips.

SPRING OUTING

A long, light and pliable braid of raffia can be used for three new ideas—
an original hat for the first sunny days, a practical shoulder bag for the hot season
and a woven basket for freshly-picked fruit.

HAT AND SHOULDER BAG

WHAT YOU NEED
APPROXIMATELY **12m (45')**
OF BRAIDED RAFFIA
FLAT RAFFIA
WOOL NEEDLE
CARDBOARD
STAPLER
SCISSORS
GLUE
HEMP OR JUTE RIBBON

Before starting on the hat, make a cylinder from the cardboard using the same circumference as your head; this will serve as a support on which to model the hat. Fasten the ends of the cardboard to each other with the stapler to complete the cylinder. If the cardboard is thin, reinforce the edges by gluing another strip of cardboard 2–3cm (³/₄–1¹/₈") wide around it.

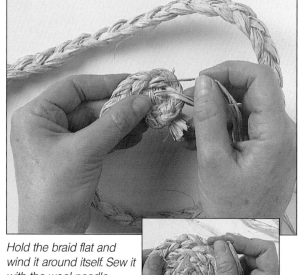

Hold the braid flat and wind it around itself. Sew it with the wool needle threaded with a strand of raffia. Distance the stitches approximately 1cm (³/₈") from each other. Continue winding the braid in a circle and sewing it until you have a disk with a diameter 3–4cm (1¹/₈"–1⁹/₁₆") smaller than that of the cardboard cylinder for the top.

Go around another two or three times, bending the braid downwards (this is to round the top down), before reaching the same circumference as the cylinder.

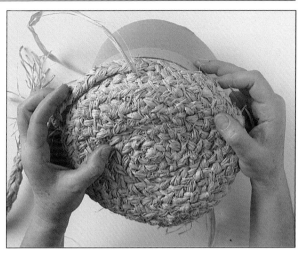

Continue vertically with the braid to form the cylindrical part of the hat, and sew it with the strand of raffia. Slip the hat over the cylinder now and again to check for evenness.

To shape the brim, sew a round of braid tilted outwards. The inclination depends on the form and size you wish to give the brim. For a small brim, the inclination should be quite marked at more than a 90–100° angle. Try to thin the braid out gradually as you come towards the end until it is finished. Secure with a few close stitches.

Use the same technique to make the shoulder bag. You will need a braid approximately 16–17m (54–56') long. For the shoulder strap, make a seven-way braid or use a broad hemp ribbon and sew it inside the bag.

BASKET

WHAT YOU NEED
17M (56') BRAIDED RAFFIA
RAFFIA AND WOOL NEEDLE
5M (16'6") CANE (DIAMETER
0.5MM, 0.02")
DOUBLE-SIDED TAPE
6M (19'9") HEMP OR JUTE
ROPE (DIAMETER 8MM, $^5/_{16}$"),
CUT INTO THREE EQUAL
LENGTHS

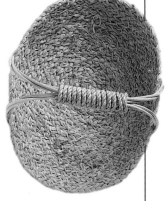

Wind the braided raffia to make a slightly concave basket 34cm (13$^5/_{16}$") in diameter. Use 2.5m (8'4") of cane for the handles; form a circle with a 28cm (11") diameter and fasten by entwining the ends. Make a second circle in the same way using the remaining cane.

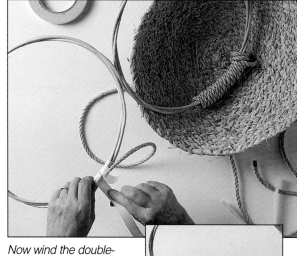

Now wind the double-sided tape for approximately 14cm (5$^5/_8$") along both cane circles and secure the ends. Cover the double-sided tape with the hemp rope— you will need approximately 2m (6'7"). To secure the initial end, place the rope on the double-sided tape and wind it round. To secure the other end, slip it under the last two rounds of rope and pull tightly.

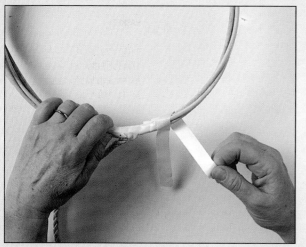

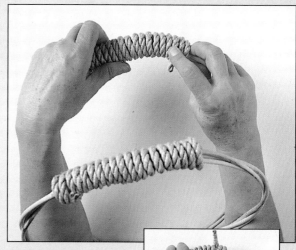

To make the handle, bring the two parts wrapped in rope together. On the diametrically opposite side, join the two circles with the double-sided tape (approximately 14cm, 5⅝"). Cover the tape with the hemp rope. The end of the rope can be secured using hot glue.

To finish, separate the unfastened sides of the two cane circles and insert the basket. Secure the circles in at least four points with needle and raffia.

WREATHS AND STARS

Summer is the time of ripe grains and their golden colors. Ideal for every corner of your home, they can be used for a variety of decorations—a sign of welcome on the door, a touch of light on the wall, or even an ornament for the Christmas tree. My favorite cereal wreath is that made with oats—thousands of newly stripped heads swaying to conjure up visions of the sun and fields. You can decorate it with a pretty ribbon or dried flowers, but it is delightful as it is—a natural pinwheel.

WHAT YOU NEED

A BASE WREATH MADE FROM
OAT STALKS
OATS
FINE WIRE
(DIAMETER 0.35MM)

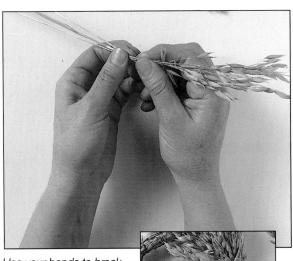

Use your hands to break the tops off the oats about 10–11cm (4–4³⁄₈") down. Use the sides of the ears as well, including seemingly less attractive ones, as you will need a great many for this decoration. Make a bunch consisting of four or five oat stalks and secure with wire to the base wreath.

Now add a second bunch tilting inwards and a third tilting outwards. Continue in this way all around the wreath. The bunches should be thick and evenly distributed. The final ones require a little more patience and care, as the fastening wire must not be visible.

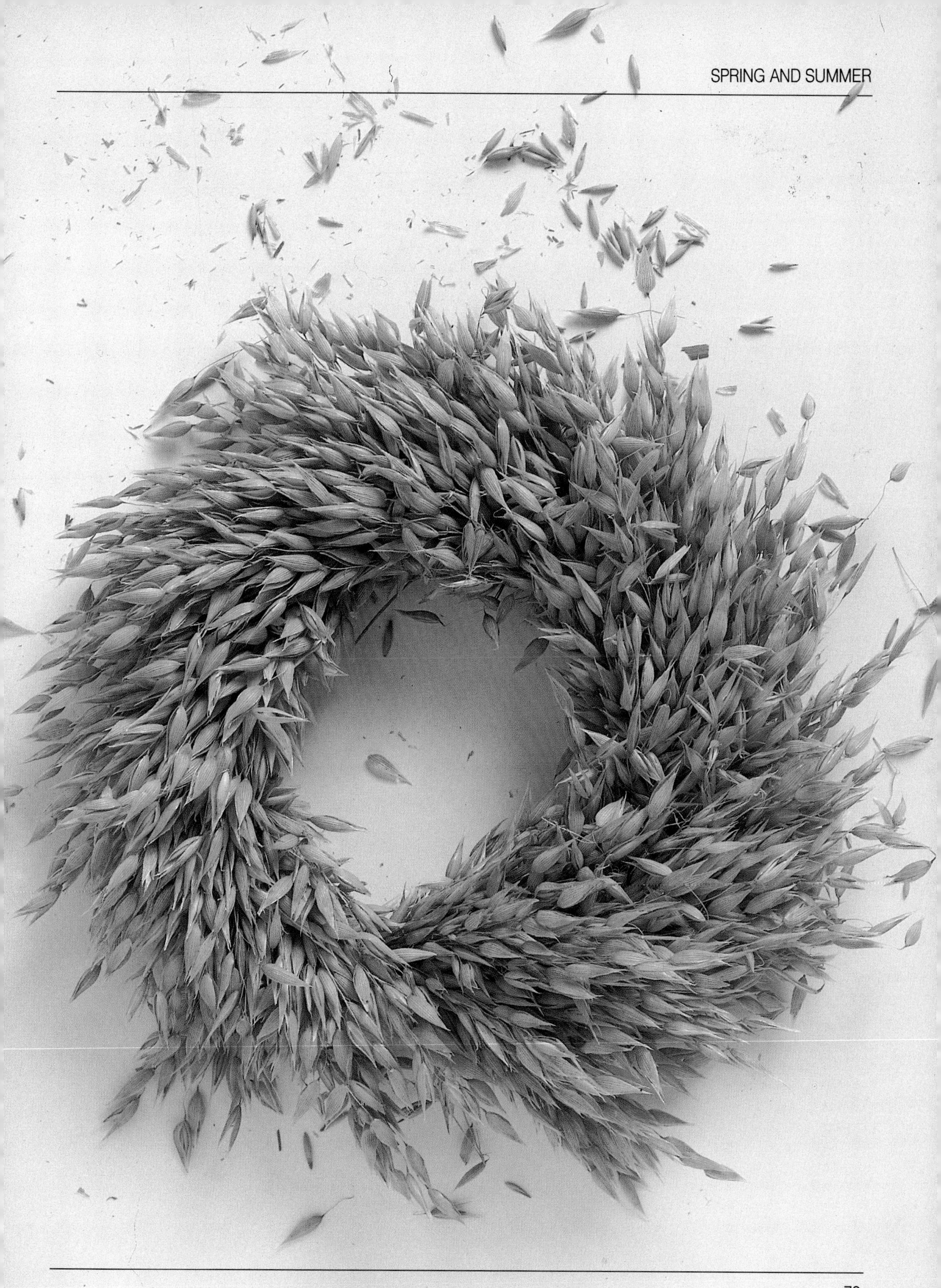

WOVEN WHEAT DECORATIONS

The method adopted for these small decorations is similar to that of the colorful key rings woven with multicolored plastic threads that were so trendy years ago. You can weave golden cereal spikes creatively to produce good luck charms to accompany a gift or greeting card.

HEART

WHAT YOU NEED
TEN BLACK SPIKES OF WHEAT
WOODEN SKEWER
RAFFIA
SCISSORS
BOWL

For these creations I use black wisps, the stalks of which are virtually knot-free. Choose the spikes with the longest stalks and leave them to soak for several hours. Always remember to work with wet hands to prevent the stalks from drying out and losing their suppleness.

Make a bunch with five spikes and tie it with raffia. Turn the spikes upside down, open them up into a star shape and insert the skewer in the center. This will help keep the weave straight and even.

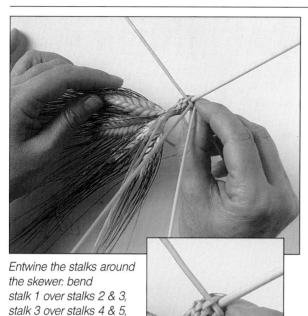

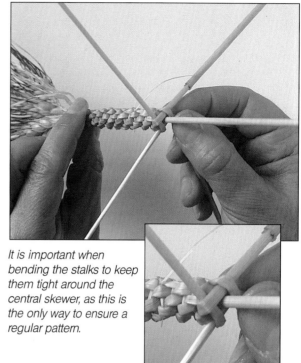

Entwine the stalks around the skewer: bend stalk 1 over stalks 2 & 3, stalk 3 over stalks 4 & 5, stalk 5 over stalks 1 & 2, and so on to the end of the stalks.

It is important when bending the stalks to keep them tight around the central skewer, as this is the only way to ensure a regular pattern.

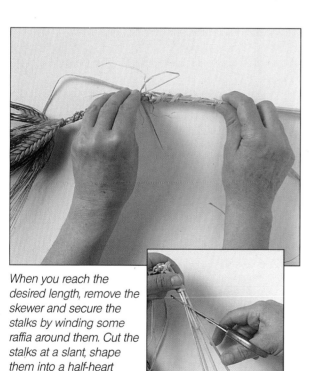

When you reach the desired length, remove the skewer and secure the stalks by winding some raffia around them. Cut the stalks at a slant, shape them into a half-heart shape and leave to dry. In the meantime, repeat the operation with the other five stalks.

Join the two halves and tie them together at the bottom and at the base of the spikes to form a heart. To do this use a strand of raffia tied in a bow in both places.

NOTEBOOK AND CARDHOLDER

An original notebook and a cardholder decorated with personal touches will make unusual and welcome gifts.
Choose clay shapes suited to the recipient to make a recipe book for the family cook,
a diary for a romantic friend or a travel log for an intrepid traveler.

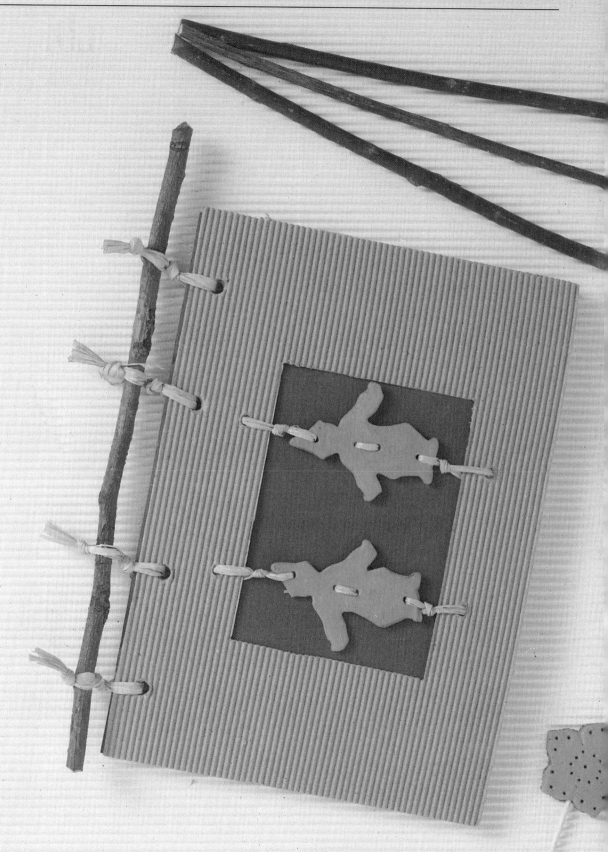

WHAT YOU NEED

NOTEBOOK
NOTEBOOK (21x15CM,
8¹/₃–6") WITH PERFORATED
PAGES
SMOOTH DARK BROWN
CARDBOARD
CORRUGATED LIGHT BROWN
CARDBOARD
POLYMER CLAY
ROLLING PIN
RAFFIA
WOODEN SKEWER
TWIG (25CM, 10")
COOKIE CUTTERS
WAXED PAPER, GLUE
CRAFT KNIFE, SCISSORS, PENCIL
PUNCH PLIERS
FINE SANDPAPER

CARDHOLDER
CORRUGATED CARDBOARD
TEMPLATE, PENCIL
TUBULAR BROWN ELASTIC
POLYMER CLAY, CRAFT KNIFE
STAR COOKIE

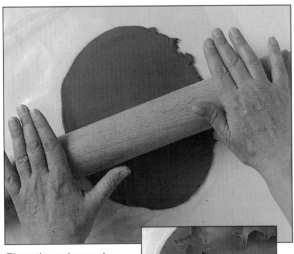

Place the polymer clay between two sheets of waxed paper and flatten with the rolling pin until it is 3mm (¹/₈") thick. Remove the top sheet of waxed paper. Press the cutters into the polymer clay and carefully remove the cut shapes.

Use the skewer to make holes in the clay for the raffia to go through. Place the shapes on the waxed paper and dry them in the sun, on a radiator or in a half-open oven at 60–70°C (140–158°F). Turn occasionally to keep flat. When they are dry, smooth the edges and holes with sandpaper.

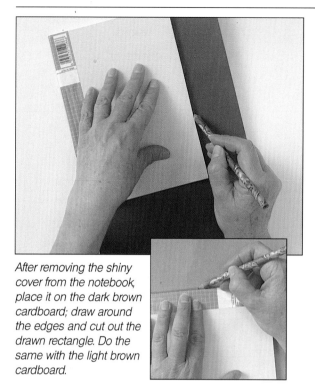

After removing the shiny cover from the notebook, place it on the dark brown cardboard; draw around the edges and cut out the drawn rectangle. Do the same with the light brown cardboard.

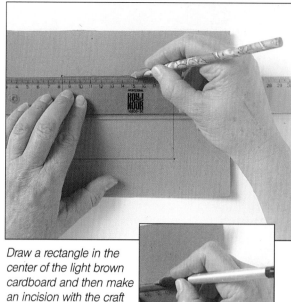

Draw a rectangle in the center of the light brown cardboard and then make an incision with the craft knife; this is the space for the chosen shapes. The size of the rectangle will depend on the size of the shapes.

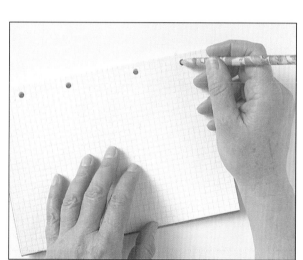

Lay the notebook on the light brown cardboard rectangle; insert a pencil into the holes and mark them on the cardboard. Use the punch pliers to make the holes. Always remember to place a piece of leather or rubber between the object to be punched and the base of the pliers. In this way the punch blade does not touch the steel pliers and the blade lasts longer.

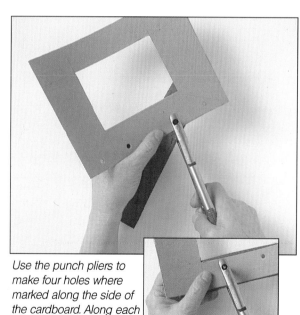

Use the punch pliers to make four holes where marked along the side of the cardboard. Along each of the longest sides of the central rectangle also make two holes to tie the shapes in place.

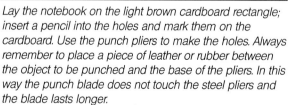

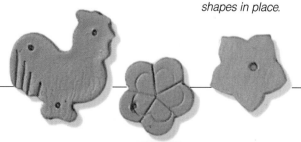

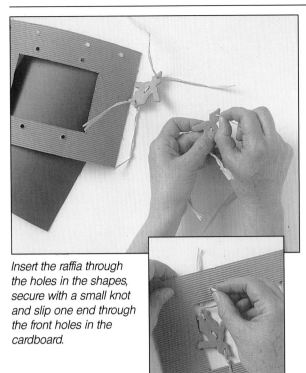

Insert the raffia through the holes in the shapes, secure with a small knot and slip one end through the front holes in the cardboard.

Bring the two ends of the raffia together on the back and secure with a little glue. Spread the glue on the inside of the two pieces of cardboard and glue them together.

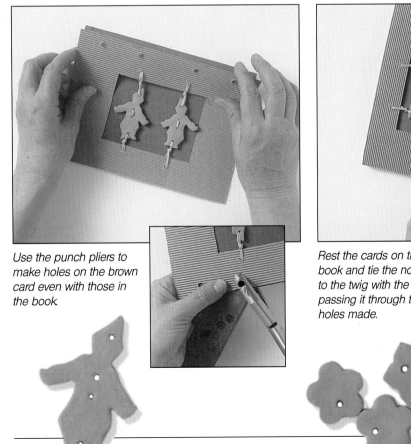

Use the punch pliers to make holes on the brown card even with those in the book.

Rest the cards on the book and tie the notebook to the twig with the raffia, passing it through the holes made.

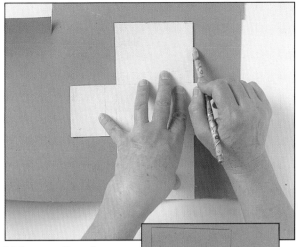

Make a cardboard template in the shape of the cardholder. Rest the template on the cardboard so that it follows the lines of the cardboard. Mark the edges and folding lines with a pencil. Use the craft knife to cut around the shape and slightly incise the fold lines on the back.

Shape the cardholder folding the cardboard along the incised lines. Make two holes in the center of the upper flap with the punch, one below the other. Leave approximately 1.5cm (⁵/₈") between the bottom hole and the edge.

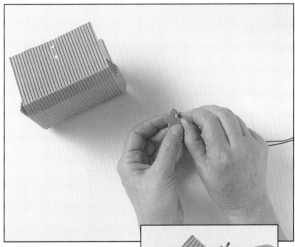

Use a cookie craft knife to make the polymer clay decoration for the fastening. Make a hole at one end and insert the round elastic, folded twice and tied at the ends. Pass the elastic through the holes in the cardboard starting from the hole closest to the edge and proceeding from back to front and vice versa.

Pass the elastic around the closed cardholder and hook onto the star-shaped button.
You can make a pencil case in the same way. The holes for the elastic should again be made at the center of the upper flap, but parallel, not perpendicular, to the longest side.

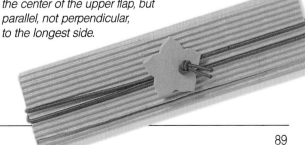

A TASTE OF THE SEA

I always come home from a seaside vacation with a suitcase full of mementos: shells, smooth driftwood, a shred of fishing net left on the rocks, the core from an Indian fig (a prickly pear cactus) stem with its delightful pattern. I have used materials gathered on the seashore together with a lovely piece of coral received as a gift some years ago to make the picture frames shown here. I hope they inspire you in your "marine" creations.

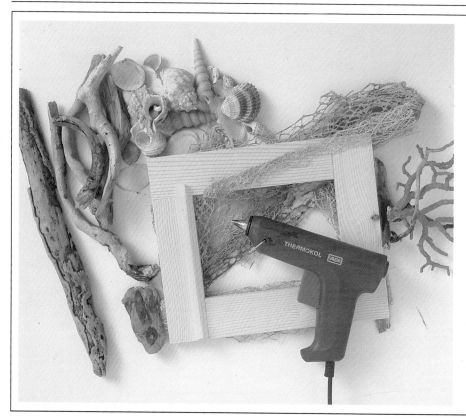

WHAT YOU NEED

UNVARNISHED WOODEN
FRAME
WEBBING FOUND INSIDE
PRICKLY PEAR CACTUS STEMS
SMOOTH DRIFTWOOD
SHELLS AND SMALL CORALS
CORAL BRANCH
HOT GLUE GUN
HACKSAW

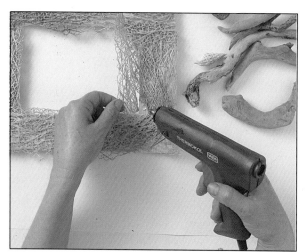

Glue the webbing from the prickly pear cactus stem all over the frame. Choose the finest pieces and do not overlap unless necessary.

Before applying the driftwood, experiment with samples adapting them to the shape of the frame. Strongly curved wood is best for the corners and straighter pieces for the sides. Start the decoration from one corner. Glue on the driftwood, only partially covering the webbing.

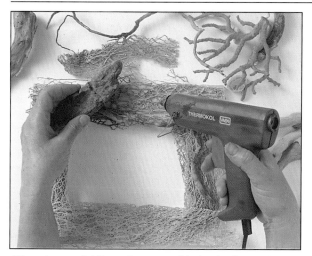

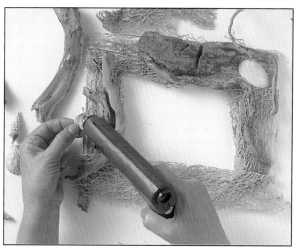

If the pieces of driftwood are too wide for the frame, they can be split lengthwise. If the wood is thin enough and is knot free, cut by inserting a fine blade at the desired breaking point and hitting it with a hammer.

When you are satisfied with the frame, glue the shells onto the spaces left between the wood, choosing the most suitable size. Pick shells worn smooth by the seawater and with incrustations in the colors and surface textures most in keeping with the rest of the decoration.

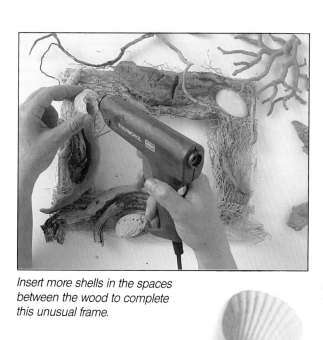

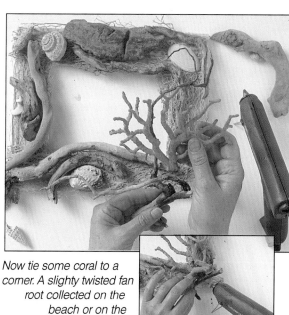

Insert more shells in the spaces between the wood to complete this unusual frame.

Now tie some coral to a corner. A slighty twisted fan root collected on the beach or on the rocks is ideal.

BY CANDLELIGHT

Summer evenings will be all the more enjoyable in the presence of candles molded inside unusual containers and decorated with the natural materials of your choice. The warm light of these candles will enliven balconies and gardens and they can be personalized with your own special touches—a rush wreath, rope, shells gathered on the seashore or some bark.

WHAT YOU NEED

A CANDLE WITH FIVE WICKS
IN A CLAY POT
THREE WILLOW BRANCHES
REEDS
FINE BROWN WIRE
SCISSORS
HOT GLUE

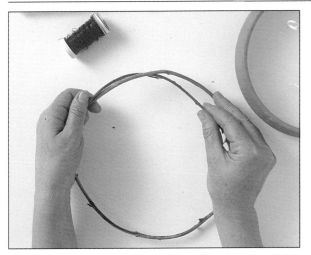

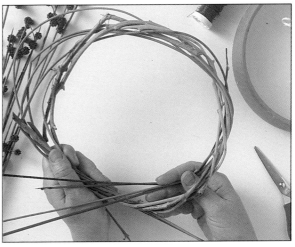

Bend a willow branch to form a ring with a diameter slightly larger than that of the clay pot. Entwine the ends and wind another two willow branches around this wreath base. Secure if necessary with a little wire.

Now start to wind the reeds around the wreath to thicken it. Use branches with few flowers for an even result.

End by entwining the stalks with the flowers, leaving the flowering ends free, and winding the rest tightly.

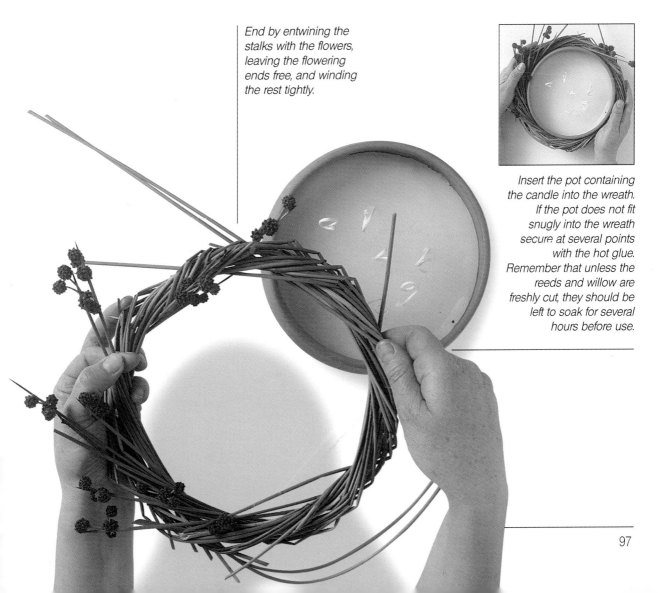

Insert the pot containing the candle into the wreath. If the pot does not fit snugly into the wreath secure at several points with the hot glue. Remember that unless the reeds and willow are freshly cut, they should be left to soak for several hours before use.

HAPPY EASTER

Eggs have always been important symbols and are particularly suitable for natural decorations.
Here, they prove surprisingly beautiful—revealing the many faces of spring impressed on the
shells by young leaves.

WHAT YOU NEED

WHITE AND BEIGE EGGS
TWO LARGE HANDFULS OF
RED ONION SKINS
(Tropea onions)
1 L (4 cups)
OF WATER
TWO PANS
A NYLON STOCKING
SCISSORS
BRASS WIRE
SYRINGE
KITCHEN TOWEL
IVY LEAVES

FOR THE EGG PREPARATION

SEWING NEEDLE
WOODEN TOOTHPICK
SANDPAPER
SYRINGE
PENCIL
VINEGAR
COLORED RIBBONS

PREPARING THE EGGS

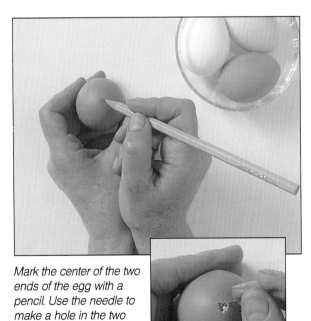

Mark the center of the two ends of the egg with a pencil. Use the needle to make a hole in the two marks and another six to eight holes at a distance of 1mm in a circle around each end.

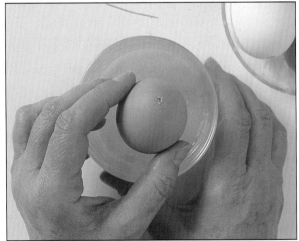

The best way to empty the egg, removing the yolk and white, is to blow quite strongly into one of the holes; in fresh eggs, in particular, the film over the yolk is quite thick. If you are unable to empty it, the hole can be enlarged slightly.

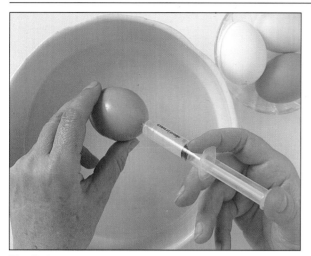

To eliminate all traces of yolk inside the shell, wash with a mixture of water and vinegar using a syringe.

To enlarge the holes, insert the needle and rotate, holding it at a slant. The shell will break evenly without cracking. Roll up a piece of sandpaper, slip it into the holes and enlarge them by sanding the edges, which will become more regular.

HANGING THEM

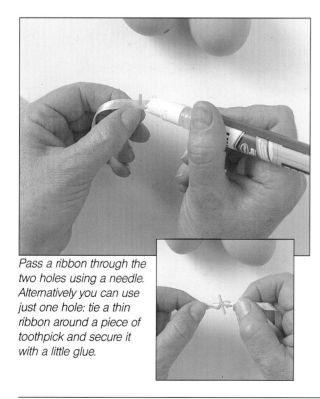

Pass a ribbon through the two holes using a needle. Alternatively you can use just one hole: tie a thin ribbon around a piece of toothpick and secure it with a little glue.

Insert the whole piece of toothpick into the hole; then, pull the ribbon gently. The toothpick will lie across the inside of the shell and the egg will be ready to hang.

Pour one liter of hot water over the onion skins and leave to soak for two hours, or even better overnight. Then, boil the skins and water for an hour and leave to rest before straining. Keep the water, which will have turned red, in a small pan.

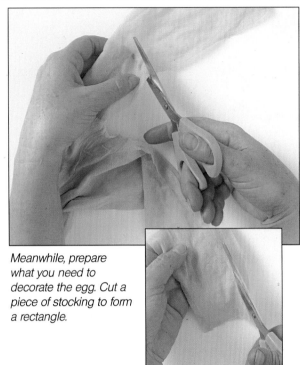

Meanwhile, prepare what you need to decorate the egg. Cut a piece of stocking to form a rectangle.

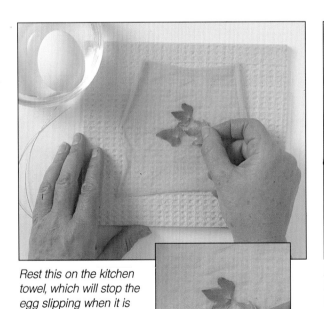

Rest this on the kitchen towel, which will stop the egg slipping when it is wrapped in the nylon. Place the small ivy leaves in the center of the stocking.

Lay a white egg (wet it for better adhesion) on the leaves. Wrap the nylon around the egg. Overlap the two sides of the rectangle as little as possible to ensure the shell absorbs the color well.

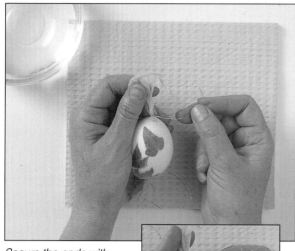

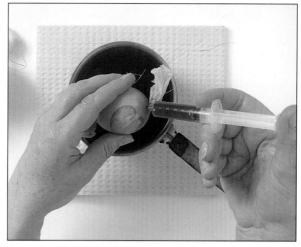

Secure the ends with some brass wire. The nylon must be taut and if possible with no folds so that the shell takes on a uniform color. Now proceed in the same way with a beige egg; this enables you to appreciate the different color effects on two types of shell.

Bring the filtered onion water to a boil and, after removing the pan from the heat, immerse the eggs in the colored water. To prevent the empty shells from floating, you can fill them beforehand with onion water using a small syringe, or you can place a light-weight object over them.

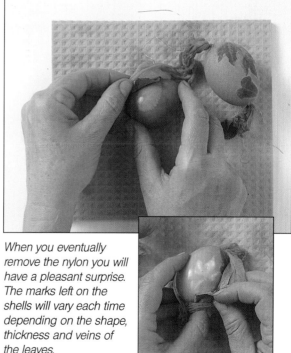

Cover the shells and leave them immersed in the dye until the water is cold. Turn them at least once during this time taking care not to move the leaves. This will allow the dye to color the eggs evenly.

When you eventually remove the nylon you will have a pleasant surprise. The marks left on the shells will vary each time depending on the shape, thickness and veins of the leaves.

PAPER EGGS

Seemingly as light as feathers, these are highly unusual but easy to make. All you need is some craft glue, scissors and brightly colored crepe paper. Place them amidst primrose flowers or hang at different heights in a window; they will bring an immediately festive Easter feel to the air.

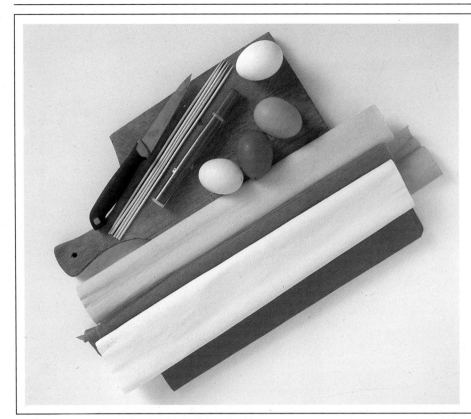

WHAT YOU NEED

EGGS
CREPE PAPER IN VARIOUS
COLORS
CHOPPING BOARD
NON-SERRATED KNIFE
SCISSORS
CRAFT GLUE
NEEDLE
WOODEN SKEWERS
EMBROIDERY THREAD

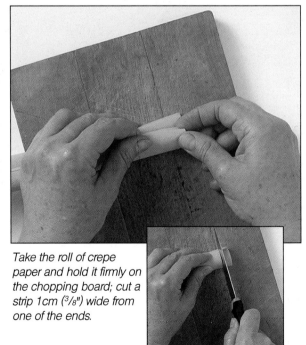

Empty the eggs of their contents by making a hole at each end and blowing the yolk and white out. Insert a skewer through one of the holes into the egg and glue it to the shell. If the hole is too big, glue a strip of paper or embroidery thread around the skewer.

Take the roll of crepe paper and hold it firmly on the chopping board; cut a strip 1cm (³/₈") wide from one of the ends.

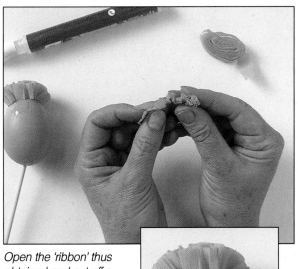

Open the 'ribbon' thus
obtained and cut off a
piece approximately
15–20cm (6–8") long; curl
and roll this up slightly to
create a decoration for the
top of the egg.

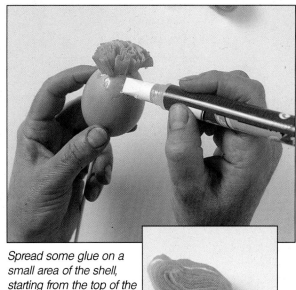

Spread some glue on a
small area of the shell,
starting from the top of the
egg. Check the quantity of
glue carefully to make sure
there is enough but not so
much that it might drip
down the shell.

Leave the glue to set for a few seconds. Place the roll of
paper vertically on the glue and hold still for a few minutes
to allow it to dry. In the meantime, prepare more rolls of
paper.

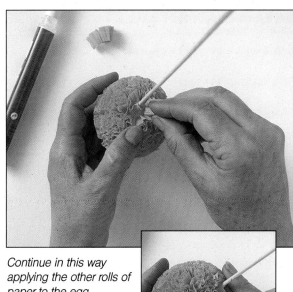

Continue in this way
applying the other rolls of
paper to the egg,
covering a small area at a
time. Make sure the last
area covered is as thick
and even as the rest.

PAPIER-MÂCHÉ GREETING CARDS

Spices, shells, date branches, twigs, raffia, jute or flowers—there is a large variety of natural materials that will add your own personal touch to the decoration of these papier-mâché cards. They can accompany a gift, be framed or used as invitations or for messages or memos. Fun and relaxing to make, just a wool needle for the raffia, a little glue and there you are!

WHAT YOU NEED

HANDMADE PAPIER-MÂCHÉ
CARD (SEE INSTRUCTIONS
ON PAGE 22)
FOUR STAR ANISE FRUITS
THREE PIECES OF CINNAMON
(2CM, $^7/_8$" LONG)
RAFFIA
WOOL NEEDLE
THREE OAT LEAVES
SCISSORS
GLUE
HACKSAW

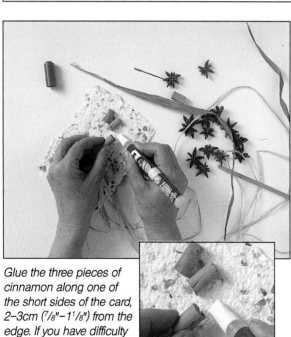

Glue the three pieces of cinnamon along one of the short sides of the card, 2–3cm ($^7/_8$"–1$^1/_8$") from the edge. If you have difficulty obtaining cut cinnamon, use a long stick cut with the hacksaw. Cut carefully, as cinnamon easily crumbles.

Thread two strands of raffia through the wool needle. Holding the card with the cinnamon at the bottom, sew four downward slanting stitches, each at least 2cm ($^7/_8$") long, down the left side starting from the top.

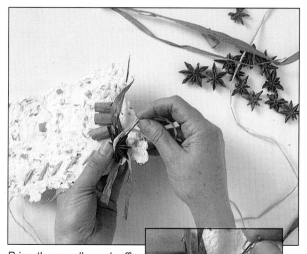

Bring the needle and raffia out in the corner between the stitches and the cinnamon. Place a star anise on three oat leaves and secure with the same raffia before slipping the needle back through the same hole. Leave the work without removing the needle.

Now prepare the string of star anise fruits for the side opposite the stitches. Pass a strand of raffia around a star anise and secure it with a side knot; tie another knot approximately 1.5cm ($^9/_{16}$") from the first and tie on a second star anise, again securing it on the side. Knot the ends of the raffia to form a small loop.

Return to the needle with the raffia and bring it out passing it beneath the pieces of cinnamon in the empty corner. Insert the loop of the string of star anise fruits.

Remove the needle and tie the two ends of the raffia in a bow around the star anise, covering the loop.

BURLAP BASKETS

Once considered humble sackcloth and seen mainly in coffee bags, burlap used to come from a distant world bearing faded wording, a few somewhat primitive designs and an aroma that stirred up dreams of distant lands. I have used it to make dried fruit baskets, but the same method can be adopted to make panels, flowerpot covers, boxes or statues.

WHAT YOU NEED

BURLAP
WALLPAPER PASTE
CARDBOARD CAKE-BASE
(DIAMETER 30CM, 12")
GLASS BOWL
SCISSORS
PUNCH
WHISK
LARGE DISH
WIRE
RAFFIA
WOODEN SKEWERS
PLASTIC WRAP

Pour a liter of water into the dish and, with the aid of the whisk, dissolve two level tablespoons of wallpaper paste in the water. Leave to set for at least half an hour, mixing occasionally. Fold the burlap twice and use the cardboard cake-base to cut two circles. Fold these into fourths and mark the center, pushing a piece of wire through.

Immerse the burlap circles in the water and paste solution in the larger dish, and soak for at least half an hour. Turn them occasionally so that they are fully saturated.

Turn the glass container upside down and cover with the plastic wrap. Spread the burlap over this centering it well. The piece of wire previously inserted will help.

Shape it around the edges, pinching it in six or seven points, at an equal distance one from the other if possible. Press it down well on the support and secure with the skewers to ensure it keeps its shape as it dries.

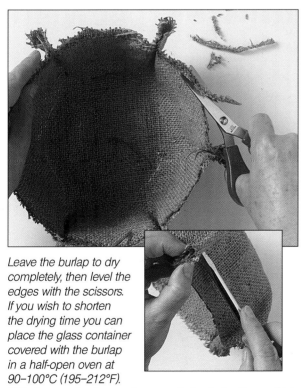

Leave the burlap to dry completely, then level the edges with the scissors. If you wish to shorten the drying time you can place the glass container covered with the burlap in a half-open oven at 90–100°C (195–212°F).
With the punch pliers, make some holes in the flaps, which were created b pinching the material.

Pass the raffia, inserted in the doubled wire, through the holes in the flaps. Knot the ends and make a bow. When making these containers, always fold the burlap twice or three times, according to the intended project. The larger the containers the more the base will have to be reinforced.

FALL-WINTER

WOODEN BOXES

Do you remember Shaker boxes? These boxes reflect the simple style and craftsmanship associated
with the religious sect known as Shakers in America during the nineteenth century.
These make beautiful presents in themselves to be used as original ornaments or as boxes for precious gifts.

WHAT YOU NEED

ONE PIECE OF BIRCH PLYWOOD
(150x20CM, 60x8"; 0.6MM
THICK)
ONE PLYWOOD DISK (13x0.8CM,
$^1/_2$ X$^1/_{32}$")
METAL RULER
MASKING TAPE
(3CM (1$^1/_8$") & 5CM (2") WIDE,
RESPECTIVELY)
TRIANGLE, PENCIL
ELASTIC (2CM ($^7/_8$") WIDE)
STAPLER, CRAFT KNIFE
FAST-ACTING WOOD GLUE
CLOTHES PINS, PUNCH PLIERS
A FEW BRASS NAILS, HAMMER
WIRE CUTTERS
MAHOGANY-BROWN WATER
STAIN
FELT-TIP PEN
GLASS BOWL
LARGE DISH
BEESWAX OR FLAT VARNISH
FINE SANDPAPER NO. 160

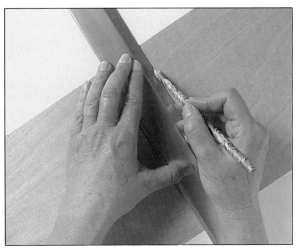

Measure out the plywood for the sides of the box and the lid. Use a ruler to find a point 47.5cm (19") from one of the shorter sides of the piece and trace a line perpendicular to the long sides. The 47.5cm (19") is then divided up as follows: 40cm (16") for the circumference of the box, 5cm (2") for the ornamental flaps and 2cm (2") for the overlap. The overlap on the lid will be shorter than that of the box as the circumference of the disk is slightly larger.

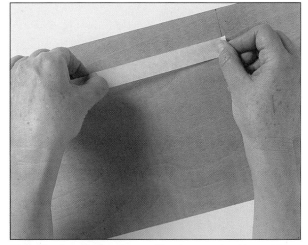

Take the 3cm ($^1/_8$") wide masking tape and cut two strips; apply these to the plywood parallel to the long side placing one 3cm ($^1/_8$") from the upper edge and the other 10cm (4") from the bottom edge. Mark the cutting lines on these two strips of tape. In this way they will be easily visible without leaving marks on the wood.

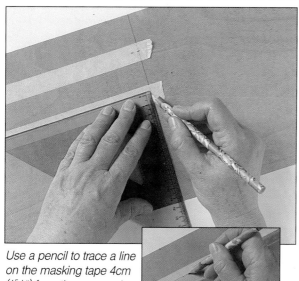

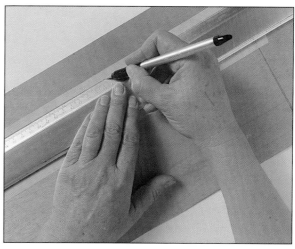

Use a pencil to trace a line on the masking tape 4cm ($1^5/_8$") from the upper edge (for the side of the lid) and one 11.5cm ($4^5/_8$") from the lower edge (for the side of the box). A strip will be left in the middle. The plywood is so divided to obtain two accurate cuts and allow for any rough edges that must be sanded away.

Holding the ruler firmly, use the craft knife along the lines marked. Proceed slowly and carefully because the blade will initially tend to follow the grain of the top layer of the plywood and this is unlikely to coincide with the pencil line. Use a metal ruler because a plastic one is easily notched and cut by the steel blade of the craft knife.

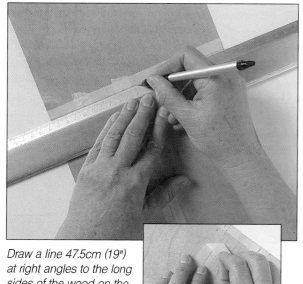

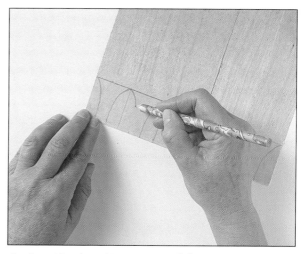

Draw a line 47.5cm (19") at right angles to the long sides of the wood on the masking tape and cut into the wood with the craft knife. Now remove the masking tape. Pass over the marked cutting lines again gently to separate the strips.

Apply a strip of masking tape 5cm (2") wide along one of the short sides of the wood. Starting from the edge of the 11.5cm ($4^5/_8$") section of the panel, draw two flaps 5cm (2") long and 3.75cm ($1^1/_2$") wide at the top. The remaining 4cm ($1^5/_8$") should be cut straight as this will be beneath the lid. Also draw a flap on the strip for the lid.

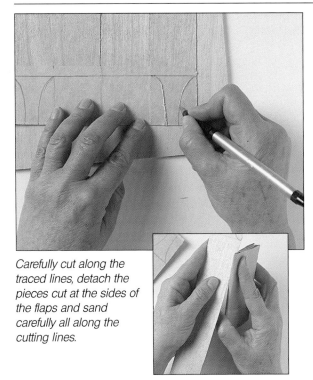

Carefully cut along the traced lines, detach the pieces cut at the sides of the flaps and sand carefully all along the cutting lines.

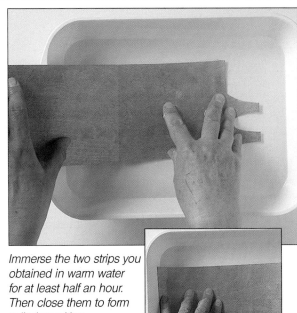

Immerse the two strips you obtained in warm water for at least half an hour. Then close them to form cylinders with a circumference equal to those of the base and the lid, respectively. Block with clothes pins. Allow these cylinders to dry out completely.

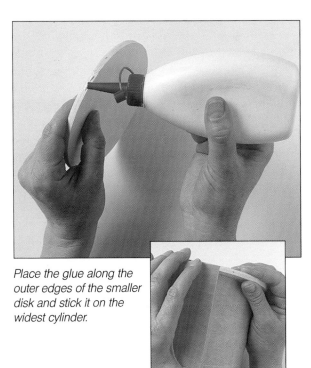

Place the glue along the outer edges of the smaller disk and stick it on the widest cylinder.

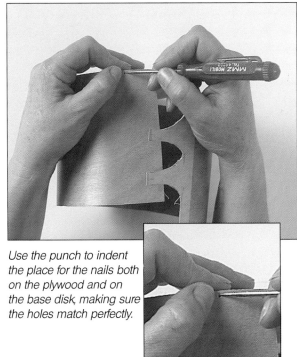

Use the punch to indent the place for the nails both on the plywood and on the base disk, making sure the holes match perfectly.

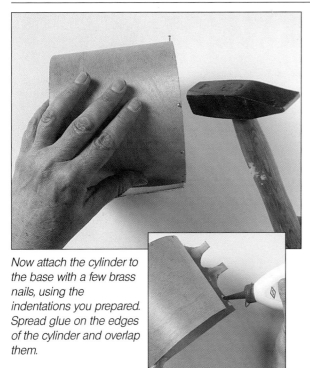

Now attach the cylinder to the base with a few brass nails, using the indentations you prepared. Spread glue on the edges of the cylinder and overlap them.

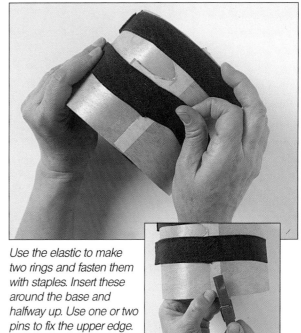

Use the elastic to make two rings and fasten them with staples. Insert these around the base and halfway up. Use one or two pins to fix the upper edge. Do the same for the lid.

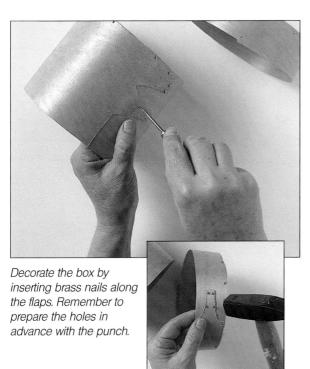

Decorate the box by inserting brass nails along the flaps. Remember to prepare the holes in advance with the punch.

Use the metal or wire cutters to cut away the tips of the nails that stick through the box. Following the instructions on the pack, dilute a small amount of water stain in half a glass of water and leave the mixture to set for at least 30 minutes. Color the box with the water stain and, when completely dry, cover with a fine layer of beeswax or flat varnish.

CHRISTMAS CENTERPIECE

Candles arranged to form a star, twigs decorated with green leaves and bright red berries—all these materials are easy to find and can be used to make a delightful centerpiece for Christmas Day.

WHAT YOU NEED

CERAMIC DISH (DIAMETER
30CM, 12")
20 CANDLES
WAX GLUE
MINERAL SPIRITS
MOSS AND IVY LEAVES
BRANCH OF DOG-ROSE WITH
RED BERRIES
WILLOW TWIGS (OR VINE,
CREEPER, HAZELNUT OR
OLEASTER SHOOTS)
RED RAFFIA
BROWN WIRE

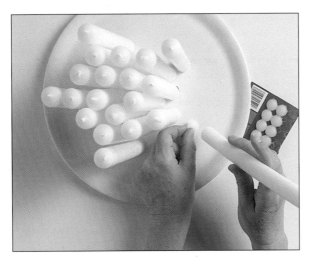

Arrange the first five candles in the center of the dish and secure with wax glue, which is easy to find in candle shops. Form another two circles of five candles each filling the spaces in the previous circle. Make sure the last five candles are aligned with those in the previous circle to form the points of a star. Remove any residue of wax glue using the blade of a knife and then a cloth soaked in mineral spirits.

Arrange the moss around the candles to completely cover the base. The candles must be of good quality—if possible, made with beeswax. Try to use candles that burn very slowly without dripping.

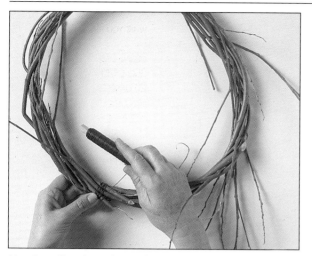

Use the willow branches to form a wreath base with the same circumference as the dish. Leave the willow to soak overnight if it is not freshly cut.

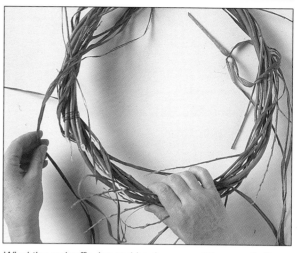

Wind the red raffia, ivy and berries around the wreath. If necessary, tie the shoots with wire.

Position the completed wreath on the dish around the candles and secure with a little wax glue.

AROMATIC CRESCENT-MOON

Made with fragrant artemisia, this original crescent-moon can also be made with lavender, broom, ivy or rosemary. The ornaments hanging from the creation can be replaced frequently with whatever your personal taste and creativity suggest.

WHAT YOU NEED

ARTEMISIA OR ROSEMARY STALKS
DRIED ORANGE PEEL AND SLICES
ORANGE PEEL STARS
APPROXIMATELY 2M (6'7")
OF RAFFIA
SELECTION OF TWIGS
BERRIES, SMALL PINE CONES AND
SPICES
PIECES OF BARK
KERNELS OF CORN
WIRE (DIAMETER 2MM)
BROWN WIRE (DIAMETER 0.35 MM)
FINE BRASS WIRE (0.30MM)
NEEDLE-NOSED PLIERS
SCISSORS AND WIRE CUTTERS
GUTTA-PERCHA
(NATURAL LATEX)
HOT GLUE

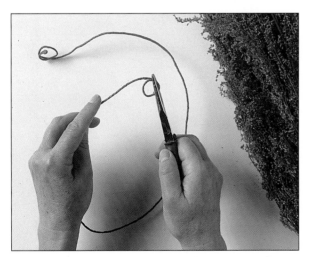

Cut approximately 70cm of wire with the wire cutter. Cover this completely with the gutta-percha (natural latex). After winding the gutta-percha around the wire a couple of times heat it between your fingers for better adhesion. Also remember to keep it taut as you perform this operation. Use the needle-nosed pliers to bend the wire at the ends and form two rings; these will be used to secure the raffia needed to hang the crescent-moon.

Tie some artemisia or rosemary around the support using the brown wire and continue until you achieve the desired thickness.

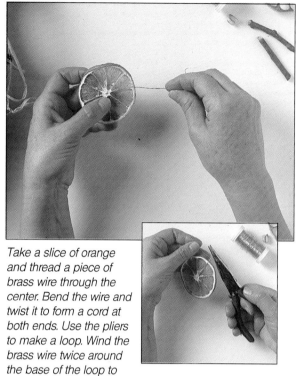

To lend greater movement to the decoration, you can add some extra twigs, tying them just at the base. Cover the wire at the ends with raffia.

Take a slice of orange and thread a piece of brass wire through the center. Bend the wire and twist it to form a cord at both ends. Use the pliers to make a loop. Wind the brass wire twice around the base of the loop to secure it and cut away the excess wire.

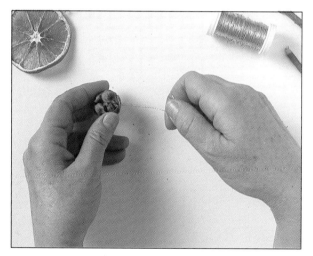

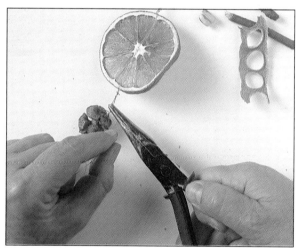

Now take a berry and tie it in the same way as with the orange, with the brass wire twisted to form a cord.

To tie the two pieces, thread the brass cord on the berry into one of the loops made on the orange slice and, using the pliers, make another loop. As for the orange, wind the brass cord several times around the base of the loop to secure it and cut away any excess wire.

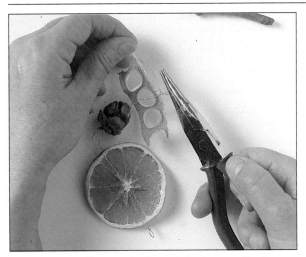

Insert a piece of brass wire through the loop on the berry and twist it around itself three times. Separate the two ends and tie a piece of orange peel onto them.

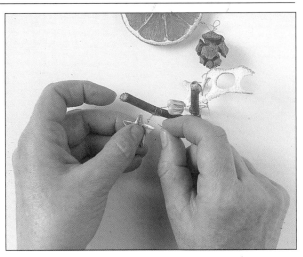

In the same way, tie a twig, two grains of maize (stuck together with a drop of hot glue), another twig and a double orange-peel star to the orange peel. Make the star with a star cookie craft knife and after cutting the two stars, stick them together leaving the colored peel on the outside.

Using this method, prepare another four mobiles using your imagination and personal taste. Cover the thicker wire with gutta-percha and use to make five hooks from which to hang the ornaments on the back of the artemisia crescent-moon.

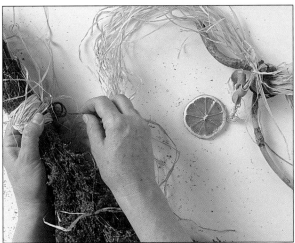

Take a bunch of raffia and tie a knot at one end. Make sure the knot is large enough not to slip through the wire ring. Pass the raffia through both crescent-moon rings and secure with another large knot. This will be used to hang it up. Decorate the center with a piece of bark and an orange mobile.

WINE BOTTLES

A bottle decorated with cane for your prized liqueur (see recipe on page 139). As well as this original bottle, the same method can be used to decorate matching jars and pots in various sizes, ideal for your homemade marmalade and raspberry jams.

WHAT YOU NEED

GLASS BOTTLE
CANE
(DIAMETER 2MM, $^1/_{16}$")
STAR ANISE
TWO SQUARES OF PLYWOOD
(5x5CM, 2x2"; THICKNESS 4MM,
$1^5/_8$") WITH TWO HOLES
ON ONE SIDE
SHEET OF PAPER
(4.5x12CM, $1^3/_8$x5")
RAFFIA
SCISSORS
WOOD GLUE

Leave the cane to soak overnight or for at least a few hours. Try to keep your hands wet as you work; this is the only way to keep the cane pliable. Twist the cane around the neck of the bottle, secure it and start to make a basket weave.

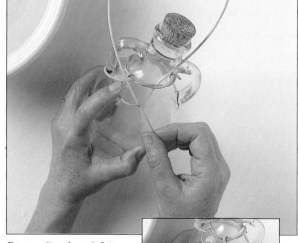

Proceeding from left to right, form an initial small arch with the cane, then make a loop passing the cane under the initial weave and proceed to form three loops. Continue in this way around the circumference of the bottle, which will require at least five or six small cane arches.

Proceed evenly, checking that all the small arches in the same row are the same size. Try to pull the loops tight as they will tend to widen as the cane dries.

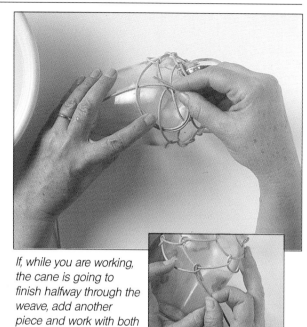

If, while you are working, the cane is going to finish halfway through the weave, add another piece and work with both for the last loops; then, proceed as normal.

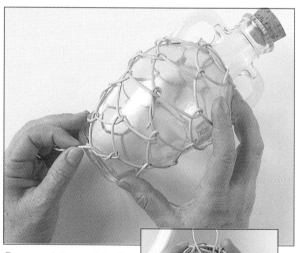

Be especially careful with the endpoint, which must be as flat and even as possible to guarantee that the bottle is stable.
Glue the last two weaves together.

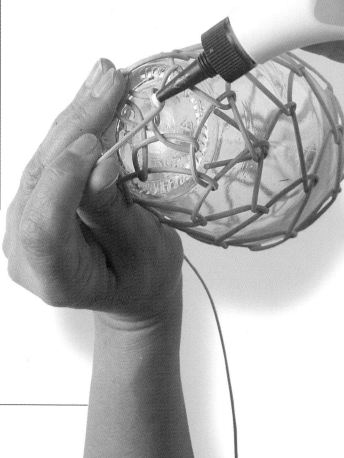

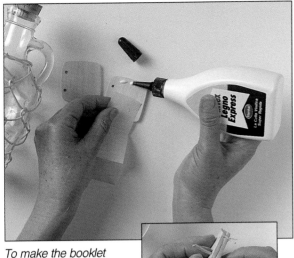

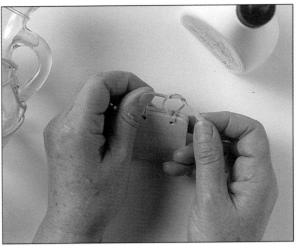

To make the booklet containing the instructions to make the liqueur, glue the sheet of paper onto one of the two plywood squares. Tie the two squares, passing a strand of raffia through the holes.

Make a knot, but leave it loose enough so that the booklet can be opened.

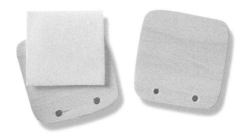

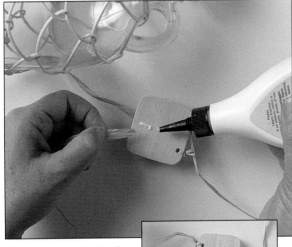

Glue two strands of raffia at the center outside of the squares and tie a bow. Cover the point where you have glued the raffia with a star anise.

Close the two covers of the booklet with a bow. Insert a strand of raffia into one of the two holes in the plywood and tie the booklet to the cane weave.

RATAFIÀ RECIPE

5g (³⁄₈oz) each of cumin, aniseed, caraway, fennel, fennel star anise and coriander seeds

Place the seeds in a mortar and crush. Put in a bottle with 1l of brandy and leave to infuse for a month. Shake the bottle every now and again. Dilute with 170g (6⁵⁄₈oz) of water boiled with 200g (8oz) of sugar. Leave to set for at least another two months.

NATURAL PICTURE FRAMES

This picture frame decorated with seeds and berries in various colors and shapes is simple to make. Enlist the help of your children and use treasures they have collected on their adventures – stones, colored pencils, or foreign coins – to personalize the picture frame.

WHAT YOU NEED

FOUR PIECES OF WOOD
(15x6CM, 6x2¹/₂")
SIX STRIPS OF WOOD WITH
A RECTANGULAR SECTION
RULER
WOOD GLUE
SANDPAPER

FOR THE DECORATION
CLOVES
NUTMEG
CARDAMOM
GINGER
CINNAMON
STAR ANISE

Use the wood glue to secure the four pieces of wood in an L-shape to form the frame.

Glue on the six strips of wood after sanding the ends; these will divide the sections to be decorated. Allow them to protrude a bit at the center of the square to hold the glass.

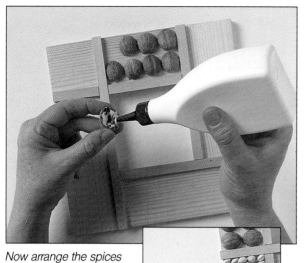

Now arrange the spices inside the squares formed, dividing them by type and securing them with a little glue. Try to position them neatly but not too perfectly. Arrange the smaller spices to look as if they have been placed casually.

The spices are to be divided by shape and color; some are white, e.g., the ginger and cardamom, others are darker and come in different shapes and sizes. Alternate them to form a harmonious ensemble.

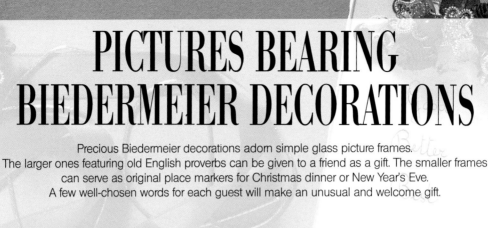

PICTURES BEARING BIEDERMEIER DECORATIONS

Precious Biedermeier decorations adorn simple glass picture frames.
The larger ones featuring old English proverbs can be given to a friend as a gift. The smaller frames
can serve as original place markers for Christmas dinner or New Year's Eve.
A few well-chosen words for each guest will make an unusual and welcome gift.

One leaf for fame,
One leaf for wealth,
One for a faithful lover
And one leaf to bring
glorious health.
Are all in a four-leaf
clover.

Sleep, baby, sleep,
Thy mother shakes the dreamland
                                    tree,
And from it fall sweet dreams
                            for thee,

        Sleep, baby, sleep -

Rain, rain, go away
Come again another
                    day -

PICTURES WITH FOUR-LEAF CLOVER

WHAT YOU NEED
18x13CM (7x5") FRAME
SEMI-RIGID BULLION (FRENCH
WIRE) (DIAMETER 1.2MM)
BULLION (DIAMETER 1.5MM)
WIRE (DIAMETER 0.35MM)
GUTTA-PERCHA (NATURAL LATEX)
THREE BULLION COILS
WITH BEAD
DECORATED CLOVES (6),
CINNAMON (2) AND STAR ANISE (1)
SIX CARDAMOM FRUITS
THREADED ON BRASS WIRE
ONE WHITE CEDAR, ONE ALDER
AND ONE JAPANESE CEDAR
BERRY
ONE ACORN CALYX
ONE GOLD TASSEL
SIX GREEN LEAVES
GREEN RIBBON
SUPERGLUE
SMALL NEEDLE-NOSED PLIERS
WHITE PAPER 18x13CM (7x5")

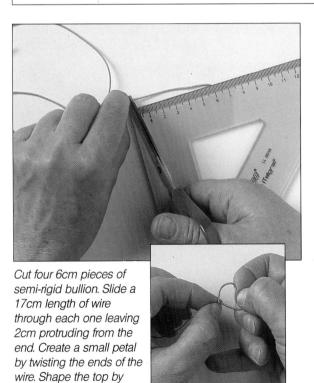

Cut four 6cm pieces of semi-rigid bullion. Slide a 17cm length of wire through each one leaving 2cm protruding from the end. Create a small petal by twisting the ends of the wire. Shape the top by bending it inwards to form a heart.

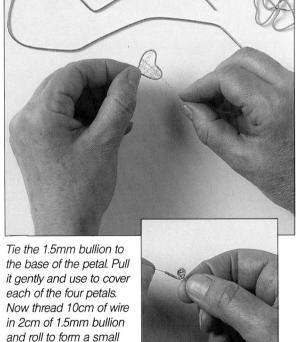

Tie the 1.5mm bullion to the base of the petal. Pull it gently and use to cover each of the four petals. Now thread 10cm of wire in 2cm of 1.5mm bullion and roll to form a small spiral shape to place at the center of the clover.

Assemble the clover and decorate it with three small green bows secured with the wire. Take a leaf, a coil of bullion and three cloves and prepare a triangular decoration. Remember to cover and secure each stalk with the gutta-percha (latex).

Now, again using the gutta-percha, add the cinnamon, Japanese cedar, another golden coil, the acorn calyx and the star anise fruit. Use the remaining spices and berries to form another smaller triangle. Hang the golden tassel at the bottom.

Use the needle-nosed pliers to twist the stalks of the two triangular decorations and the clover in a spiral. Place some superglue at the base of the largest decoration and fix to the upper side. Secure the triangle with the tassel to the left side of the glass and the clover in the top left-hand corner, arranging them to hide the stalks.

One leaf for fame,
One leaf for wealth,
One for a faithful lover
And one leaf to bring
glorious health.
Are all in a four-leaf
clover.

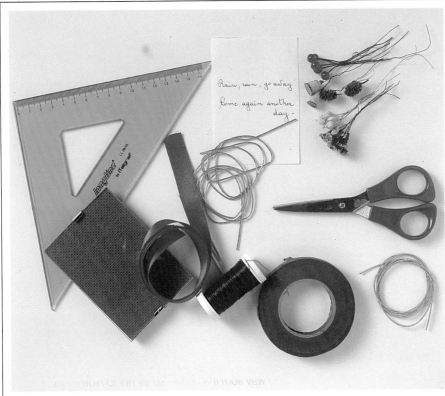

PICTURE WITH RED BERRIES

WHAT YOU NEED
SMALL FRAME
SHEET OF WHITE PAPER
(18x13CM, 7x5")
SEMI-RIGID BULLION (DIAMETER
1.2MM)
BULLION (DIAMETER 1.5MM)
WIRE (DIAMETER 0.35MM)
RED RIBBON
SIX DECORATED CLOVES
SIX CARDAMOMS
TWO ELDERBERRIES
TWO PREPARED POPPIES
FIVE-SIX SMALL RED BERRIES
GUTTA-PERCHA (NATURAL LATEX)
SCISSORS
WOODEN TOOTHPICK
SUPERGLUE
TRIANGLE OR RULER

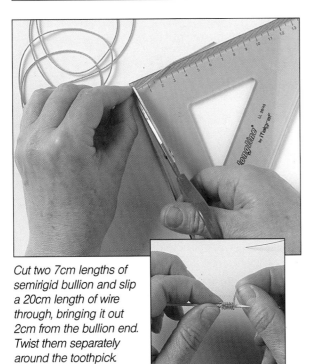

Cut two 7cm lengths of semirigid bullion and slip a 20cm length of wire through, bringing it out 2cm from the bullion end. Twist them separately around the toothpick.

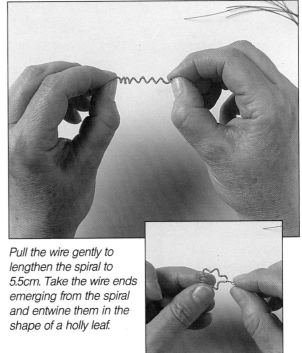

Pull the wire gently to lengthen the spiral to 5.5cm. Take the wire ends emerging from the spiral and entwine them in the shape of a holly leaf.

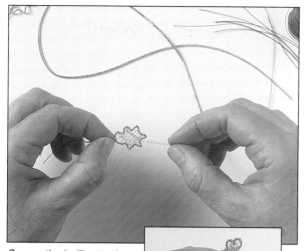

Secure the bullion to the stalk and, pulling gently but evenly, wind it around the leaf you created. Proceed in the same way for the other leaf. Place a red berry at the center of the two leaves and twist the stalks together. Cover the wire with gutta-percha (latex).

Divide the spices and berries to form two small triangular decorations, securing and covering the stalks with gutta-percha. Add the holly leaf with the gutta-percha to one of the two decorations. Secure a little way from the berries so as not to hide them.

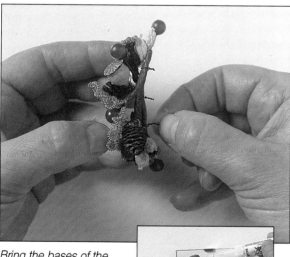

Bring the bases of the two triangular decorations together to form a single long decoration and tie on the back at three points with the wire. If the stalks are too long, cut to size. Glue the decoration to the top of the frame and apply a small red Christmas bow or two holly leaves to the bottom.

WOODEN FLOWERPOT HOLDERS

With their rustic and unusual appearance, these look as if they have come straight out of a log cabin. Made from twigs tied firmly together, wooden flowerpot holders are particularly good decorations for a mountain hut. You need little more to make them than a few twigs, some wire and a drill—you could even do it with the children after a walk in the woods.

WHAT YOU NEED

HAZELNUT, CHERRY
OR FIR TWIGS
6x15CM LENGTHS OF WIRE
(DIAMETER 1.5MM)
FINE WIRE
VICE
MANUAL DRILL
NEEDLE-NOSED PLIERS
MOSS
TWO FLOWERPOTS
HEMP ROPE
(DIAMETER 8MM, 5/16")
SCISSORS

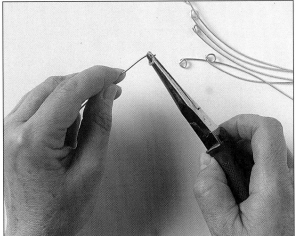

Secure the twigs in the vice and cut six 30cm (12") lengths and six 20cm (8") ones. Make holes in them 2cm (8") from the end with the drill after securing them in the vice. Also make a hole at the center of the longest ones. Make sure the holes on each twig go in the same direction. Use the needle-nosed pliers to make some small rings at one end of each of the six lengths of wire.

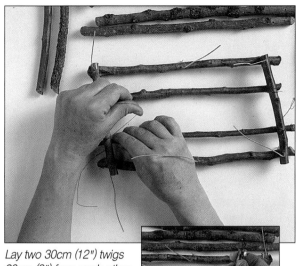

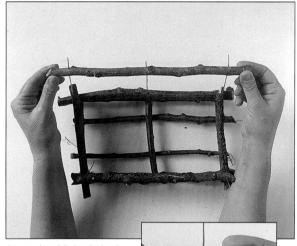

Lay two 30cm (12") twigs 20cm (8") from each other. Slip three lengths of wire into the three holes in each twig. Insert two 20cm (8") twigs at right angles. Now use the fine wire to tie two 30cm (12") twigs parallel to the first ones, beneath the two shortest twigs, to form a base for the flowerpots.

Insert the third twig in the center and tie to the two reinforcing ones. Insert another two long twigs, three short ones and two long ones.

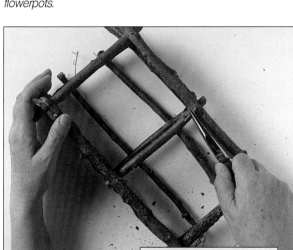

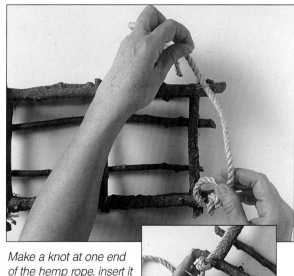

Secure the wire at the center of the twigs, bending it with the pliers toward the inside of the flowerpot holder. Bend each end of the four side wires into a ring.

Make a knot at one end of the hemp rope, insert it in two rings along the short side of the holder, secure with a knot and cut. Do the same on the other short side. Cover the bottom with moss, place the flowerpots over this base and arrange the moss around them.

LADIES AND GENTLEMEN

Quite different from the previous objects, this checkerboard is remarkably original.
Painstakingly made with attention to the minutest detail, it could be a charming ornament for
your home or a welcome gift for a checker player or a couple who like to pass
their winter evenings playing a nice traditional game.

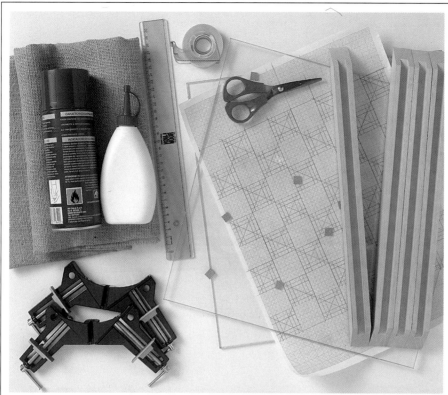

WHAT YOU NEED

FOUR STRIPS
(3x40CM, 1¹/₈"–16")
OF U-GROOVED WOOD
(10x11MM, ³/₈" –⁷/₁₆"
GROOVING)
TWO SHEETS OF GLASS
(36x36CM, 14x14")
SHEET OF GRAPH PAPER
BURLAP
PENCIL
RULER
SCISSORS
WOOD GLUE
TRANSPARENT,
DOUBLE-SIDED TAPE
CORNER CLAMPS FOR FRAMES
SPRAY GLUE

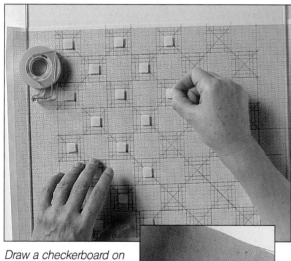

Draw a checkerboard on a sheet of graph paper with squares 3.5x3.5cm (1³/₈"x1³/₈"); each side must have eight squares. Cut the checkerboard out and place it centrally beneath one of the sheets of glass. Apply a piece of double-sided tape to the center of each square. Spray both sides of the burlap with glue.

Wait until the glue has dried and you will be able to cut it without it fraying or sticking to the scissors. Cut 32 burlap squares 3.5x3.5cm (1³/₈ x1³/₈") in size. As burlap shows the difference between warp and weft, make sure you always apply the squares onto the double-sided tape on the same side; this small attention to detail will greatly improve the effect of the whole.

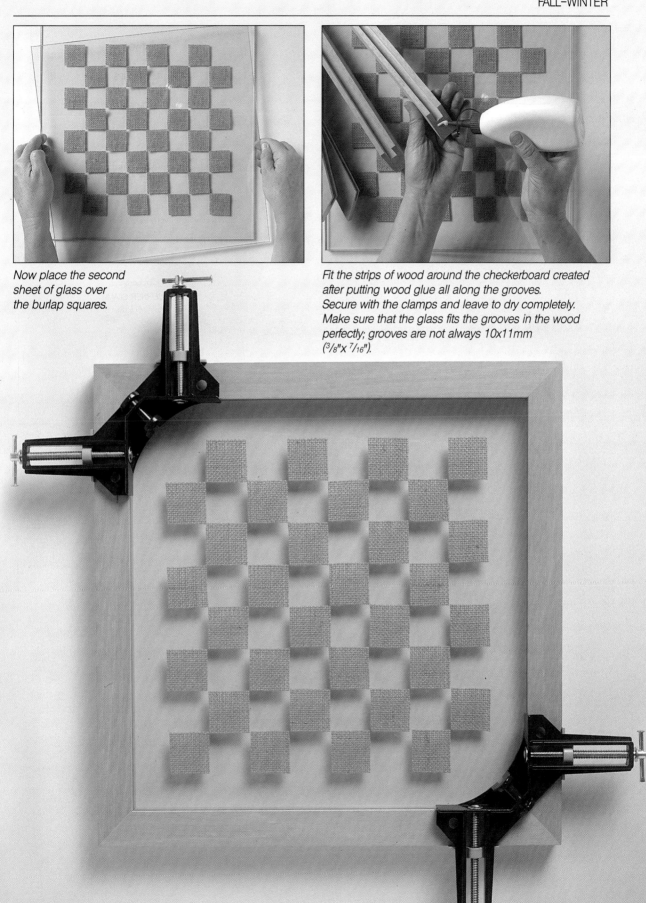

Now place the second
sheet of glass over
the burlap squares.

Fit the strips of wood around the checkerboard created
after putting wood glue all along the grooves.
Secure with the clamps and leave to dry completely.
Make sure that the glass fits the grooves in the wood
perfectly; grooves are not always 10x11mm
($^3/_8$"x $^7/_{16}$").

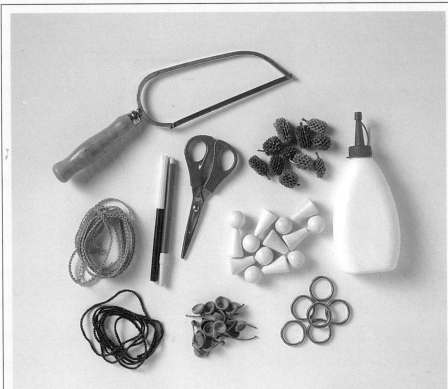

FOR THE CHECKERS

WHAT YOU NEED
24 WOODEN SHAPES
(5CM, 2" HIGH)
GOLD BRAID
BROWN CORD
12 HALF IRONWOOD BERRIES
12 ACORN CALYXES
RED FELT PEN
BLACK FELT PEN
VINYL GLUE
SIX METAL RINGS
(DIAMETER 3CM, 1 1/8")

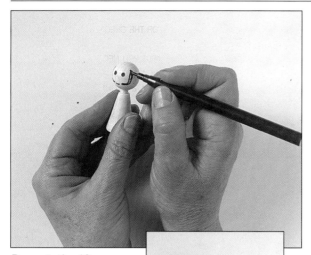

Decorate the 12 gentlemen shapes. Draw the mouth with the red felt pen and the eyes and sideburns or moustache with the black one. Dress the body by wrapping it in brown cord.

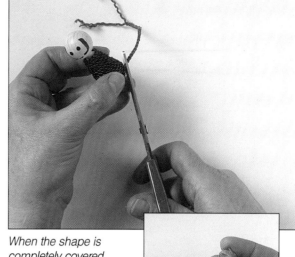

When the shape is completely covered, secure the cord with a drop of glue. Make the hat with the acorn calyx pushed well down on the forehead and secured with glue.

Now make the ladies. The face will be softer, with a heart-shaped mouth, closed eyes and a cascade of black curls.

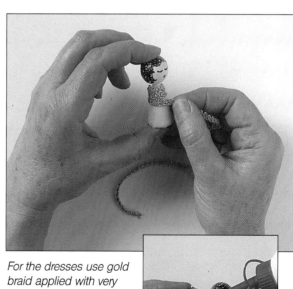

For the dresses use gold braid applied with very little glue. Use a half ironwood berry for the hat, which is almost a crown for these slightly snobbish little ladies. When you play, a brass ring slipped over the head will differentiate the kings from the normal checkers.

One leaf for fame,
One leaf for wealth,
One for a faithful lover
And one leaf to bring
glorious health.
Are all in a four-leaf
clover.

Craft Suppliers

United States:

Many natural materials can be found in your own backyard. Most craft materials can be found at your local art or craft supply store. Some national chains include:

Hobby Lobby
7707 SW 44th Street
Oklahoma City, OK 73179
Tel: (405) 745-1100
Web site: http://www.hobbylobby.com

Michaels Arts & Crafts
8000 Bent Branch Drive
Irving, TX 75063
Tel: (214) 409-1300
Web site: http://www.michaels.com

Leading U.S. Mail-order Art Suppliers:

Art Supply Warehouse (ASW Express)
5325 Departure Drive
Raleigh, NC 27616-1835
Toll Free: 1-800-995-6778
Fax: 1-919-878-5075
Web site: http://www.aswexpress.com

Dick Blick Art Materials
P.O. Box 1267
695 US Highway 150 East
Galesburg, IL 61402-1267
Toll Free: 1-800-828-4548
Fax: 1-800-621-8293
Web site: http://www.dickblick.com

Flax Art & Design
240 Valley Drive
Brisbane, CA 94005-1206
Toll Free: 1-800-343-3529
Fax: 1-800-352-9123
Web site: http://www.flaxart.com

Also try:

Home Depot, U.S.A., Inc.
2455 Paces Ferry Road
Atlanta, GA 30339-4024
Tel: (770) 433-8211
Web site: http://www.homedepot.com
Home improvement store with more than 1000 locations in the United States, Canada and internationally. Check the Store Locator on their web site for the nearest location.

Canadian Art Supplies:

CraftCo Industries, Inc.
410 Wentworth Street North
Hamilton, Ontario
Canada L8L 5W3
Web site: http://www.craftco.com